Options Trading Crash Course

How to Start Earning Passive Income in 7 Days

By Following Expert-Approved Step-By-Step

Strategies Even if You Are a Complete Beginner

Adam Buffett – Warren Jones

© **Copyright 2020** by Adam Buffett and Warren Jones.

All right reserved.

The work contained herein has been produced with the intent to provide relevant knowledge and information on the topic described in the title for entertainment purposes only. While the author has gone to every extent to furnish up to date and true information, no claims can be made as to its accuracy or validity as the author has made no claims to be an expert on this topic. Notwithstanding, the reader is asked to do their own research and consult any subject matter experts they deem necessary to ensure the quality and accuracy of the material presented herein.

This statement is legally binding as deemed by the Committee of Publishers Association and the American Bar Association for the territory of the United States. Other jurisdictions may apply their own legal statutes. Any reproduction, transmission or copying of this material contained in this work without the express written consent of the copyright holder shall be deemed as a copyright violation as per the current legislation in force on the date of publishing and subsequent time thereafter. All additional works derived from this material may be claimed by the holder of this copyright.

The data, depictions, events, descriptions and all other information forthwith are considered to be true, fair and accurate unless the work is expressly described as a work of fiction. Regardless of the nature of this work, the Publisher is exempt from any responsibility of actions taken by the reader in conjunction with this work. The Publisher acknowledges that the reader acts of their own accord and releases the author and Publisher of any responsibility for the observance of tips, advice, counsel, strategies and techniques that may be offered in this volume.

Table of Contents

Introduction	vii
Chapter 1: Important Concepts to Understand	1
What Are Options?	1
What Are Stocks?	4
What Is a Broker?	7
How Is Option Price Determined?	9
How to Read Options Quote?	13
Chapter 2: Getting Into the Mindset of an Option Trader	15
Strategies to Think Like an Option Trader	15
Important Traits of a Successful Options Trader	21
How to Determine the Right Time to Buy or Sell?	26
Chapter 3: Buying and Selling Call Options	31
What Are Call Options?	31
What Is a Long Call Strategy?	35
Which Traders Use This Strategy?	36
What Are the Advantages of This Strategy?	36
How to Effectively Use This Strategy to Generate Profits?	39
An Example of the Long Call Strategy	43
Chapter 4: Buying and Selling Put Options	45
What Are Put Options?	45
What Is a Long Put Strategy?	47
Which Traders Use This Strategy?	48
What Are the Advantages of This Strategy?	48
How to Effectively Use This Strategy to Generate Profits?	51
An Example of the Long Put Strategy	55

Chapter 5: Covered Call Strategy — 59

What Is a Covered Call Strategy? — 59
Which Traders Use This Strategy? — 60
What Are the Advantages of This Strategy? — 60
How to Effectively Use This Strategy to Generate Profits? — 62
An Example of This Strategy — 66
What Is the Risk/Reward In This Strategy? — 67

Chapter 6: Protective Put Strategy — 71

What Is a Protective Put Strategy? — 71
Which Traders Use This Strategy? — 72
What Are the Advantages of This Strategy? — 73
How to Effectively Use This Strategy to Generate Profits? — 74
An Example of This Strategy — 78
What Is the Risk/Reward In This Strategy? — 79

Chapter 7: Straddle Strategy — 81

What Is a Straddle Strategy? — 81
What Is the Long Straddle Strategy? — 82
Which Traders Use This Strategy? — 85
What Are the Advantages of This Strategy? — 85
How to Effectively Use This Strategy to Generate Profits? — 87
An Example of This Strategy — 88
What Is the Risk/Reward In This Strategy? — 89

Chapter 8: Strangle Strategy — 91

What Is a Strangle Strategy? — 91
What Is a Long Strangle Strategy? — 91
Which Traders Use This Strategy? — 93
What Are the Advantages of This Strategy? — 93
How to Effectively Use This Strategy to Generate Profits? — 95

| *An Example of This Strategy* | *97* |
| *What Is the Risk/Reward In This Strategy?* | *98* |

Chapter 9: Bonus Strategies Explained — **99**

LEAPS	*99*
Iron Condor	*104*
Bull or Bear Spread	*110*
Married Put	*114*
Protective Collar Strategy	*116*

Chapter 10: Common Mistakes Beginners Make and How to Avoid Them — **123**

Not Having a Trading Plan	*123*
Believing In the One-Size-Fits-All Concept	*125*
Ignoring the Expiration Date	*126*
Overleveraging the Trades	*128*
Error In Position Sizing of Your Trades	*129*
Buying Options Based On Whether They Are Cheap or Not	*130*
Lack of Knowledge Regarding Early-Assigned Options	*132*
Not Using the Concept of Probability	*133*
Facing Loss Because You Chose to Stay In a Written Option	*134*
You Double Up to Cover Your Losses	*136*
Not Having an Exit Strategy	*137*
Trading Options That Are Illiquid	*138*

| **Conclusion** | **141** |
| **Glossary** | **143** |

Introduction

Congratulations on purchasing Options Trading Crash Course, and thank you for doing so.

The following chapters will discuss various aspects of options trading and give you a crash course on how you can make money with options trading. It's true that when we talk about growing your money in the stock market, what most people think about is that they are going to do it with stocks, but the stock market is not all about stocks. There are options too. Options are basically contracts with the help of which you can either call or put an underlying asset at a certain price and within a fixed time period. Although, you have to remember that there is no obligation on the bearer that they have to put or call the asset.

Options are a certain class of assets, just like ETFs, bonds, stocks, and so on. But as you read this book, you will come to know of the several ways in which investing in options is so much better than any other kind of asset class. Your portfolio is going to be benefitted in so many positive ways if you choose to include options in it. Based on the current market situation you are in, options can give you leverage and also more income. I know you might be having a lot of questions in your mind right now regarding options trading, and I can assure you that all of them are going to be answered in this book.

There are plenty of books on this subject on the market, thanks again for choosing this one! Every effort was made to ensure it is full of as much useful information as possible, please enjoy!

Chapter 1: Important Concepts to Understand

Before we go into the details and strategies and all those fun parts, you have to learn some basic concepts regarding options trading, and that is what the first chapter is going to be about. Once you get to know these key points, the rest of the facts will come off as easy.

What Are Options?

When you are in the stock market, options are exactly what their term means – choice. It is a choice that you, as an investor, get in the form of a securities contract. They are basically derivatives, and their underlying securities can be anything starting from stocks to ETFs. With the help of this contract, you basically earn yourself the right to buy or sell the underlying security. But in case you choose not to sell or buy the underlying security, it will be your choice – you are not obliged to do anything.

These contracts are considered to be very versatile. There is both a seller and a buyer involved when we

Chapter 1: Important Concepts to Understand

are talking about options. In order to get ownership of the rights that the contract is providing, the buyer has to pay a certain amount of premium. Now, there are two types of options – the call options and the put options. We are going to discuss both of these in detail in the latter part of this book but now, for the sake of this discussion, let me give you a brief intro –

- With the help of the call options, you (as the holder) will get the right to buy the asset within a particular expiration date at a specific price.
- With the help of the put options, you (as the holder) will get the right to sell the asset within a particular expiration date at a specific price.

There is a bearish seller and a bullish buyer for every call option, and similarly, there is a bullish seller and a bearish buyer for every put option.

No matter what the underlying security is, usually, 100 shares of that security is what the options contracts stand for. And if you want this contract, then you will have to pay a fee in order to acquire it. Let us see an example –

Suppose you find out that you have to pay a premium of 25 cents for every contract; then, if you want to purchase an option, then it will cost you 100 x $.25 = $25.

Now, there is another term that you should know about, and it is called the strike price. The premium that you are paying depends on this strike price. So, what is this strike price? Well, it is the price at which you either sell or buy the underlying security before the said expiration date. Remember, when I told you at the beginning of this chapter that you have to exercise your right to buy or sell an option before a certain date? Well, that date is called the expiration date. It is somewhat like the expiry date on foods within which they have to be consumed. But the expiration date, in this case, depends on the underlying asset of the options you have. For example, it is usually the third Friday in the month of the contract for stocks.

There are numerous reasons for which investors and traders sell or buy options. You will actually be holding a leveraged position through options speculation, and the cost will be much lower if you compare it to that of buying shares of that particular asset directly. Another reason for choosing options is that they help in managing the risk of your portfolio and also come of great help in hedging.

Another fact that you should know about is that if you are trading in European options, then you can exercise them only on the exercise date or the expiration date, but in the case of the American options, you can exercise them any time you want, but within the expiration date.

What Are Stocks?

Well, some of you may probably know what stocks are, but I am going to explain it here again so that I can show you the difference between stocks and options. If you are a beginner who is looking forward to fulfilling some goal or you want to test your hand in the stocks market, then stocks are definitely one of the best financial instruments that you can start with. Do you know why it is stocks and not any other asset that is advised to beginners? It is because they are very simple to deal with. You buy stocks, and then you sell them in the future when the price is higher than what you bought it for. When you buy stocks, you actually get direct ownership of a part that is represented by the stocks in that company.

Stocks will definitely be a win-win for you if your ultimate goal is a long-term one because of the very straightforward approach, and you do not have too many expenses involved. All you need to do is research them in the beginning, make sure you are investing in a good company with a proper potential for growth and once the investment is done, you do not have to keep checking on the stocks every now and then. If you are using an online broker, then you can set alerts, or you can take a look at them once a year.

Now, let us talk about some of the risks that you might be facing with stocks. Well, they are pretty straightforward and simple. In case it happens that the price of the stock drops to zero, you will be losing all the money that you had invested in it. The volatility of the stocks is why it is considered to be a long-term investment where you will not need your money in the coming five years or more.

But if you are someone who is looking for a bit more flexibility, then it is options that you should be

Chapter 1: Important Concepts to Understand

looking at. They even have a smaller amount of initial investment than stocks. The time period of investment becomes less with options as compared to stocks because of the presence of that expiration date. So, if you are more inclined towards your freedom to do frequent trades, then options are going to be your favorite.

The investing process in the case of options is definitely more complex if you compare it with stocks especially because there are three things that you have to look out for and they are –

- The direction in which the stock is going move

- When exactly that move is going to happen, that is, a definite time frame prediction
- The magnitude of the move or how much the price is going to deviate from what it is now

What I stated above is basically the simplest form of how options trading is done, and as you read this book, you will understand that there are much more complex things to learn about the process. But don't worry, I am going to show you everything in a step-by-step manner.

Moreover, there are a lot of new terms that you are going to learn with options trading, some of which have already been explained like the expiration date and strike price. It is because of such a vast range of terminology that some people find options trading confusing as compared to that of stocks, but this notion will be erased once you read this book. It's true that there is a lot to learn, but the process is not difficult. Moreover, you will also learn how you can actually treat options as a form of insurance in case you are going to invest for the long-term.

What Is a Broker?

When you are trading securities, a broker is a body that acts as the intermediary between you and the exchange. This is because, in order to place any orders at the exchange, you have to be a member of it, and so if you are an individual looking forward to trading or investing at the securities exchange, you have to take the help of a broker. There are several ways in which a broker is compensated. They can be paid by the exchange itself, or separate fees, or commissions.

Chapter 1: Important Concepts to Understand

Let us move on to some more information about what brokers can do for you. They can even provide you with market intelligence, in-depth research on the type of securities you are investing in or are trading with, and also investment plans to meet your goals. Previously, there was a norm that if you wanted to invest in the stock market, you had to be rich in order to approach a broker. But from the time that online brokerages came into existence, it has become much easier and cost-effective. There are so many discount brokers who will allow you to invest or trade at lower costs, but yes, with them, you are not going to get any type of personalized advice. If you can invest a bit more money, then you can approach the full-service brokers, you will be providing you solutions and services perfectly tailored to cater to your needs.

Now, let me give you a clear picture of full-service brokers vs. discount brokers. The commission that is charged by discount brokers is towards the lower range, something between $5 and $15 for every trade, but you are not going to get any type of investment advice from them. In fact, in place of a commission, the brokers kind of receive a salary. They will also provide you with a trading platform. On the other hand, with the full-service brokers, you are going to get things like retirement planning, advice on investment options, market research, and so on, along with a lot of investment products. But if you want to execute your trades with them, you will also have to pay a higher commission. Depending on the trading volume conducted by a broker, they are paid by the firm. They also get paid whenever they sell any investment product. But in the case of services like managed investment accounts, there might be a fee-based system.

The regulatory body of brokers is termed as FINRA or Financial Industry Regulatory Authority. There is a suitability rule that is set by this body, and this rule is also responsible for holding up the brokers to a code of conduct with their clients.

How Is Option Price Determined?

Before you start trading options, one of the most basic things that you have to understand is how the options are priced and on what basis is this pricing done. There are several factors that determine the price of options like the expiration date, its intrinsic value, dividends, the current stock price, interest rates, and volatility.

Chapter 1: Important Concepts to Understand

In order to find this price, there are different models that are followed, and the most common one of them all is the Black-Scholes model, but there are also the trinomial and binomial models.

Now, let us see in what ways the different factors are affecting the price of an option.

- **Current Stock Price** – A call option will have a greater worth when the price increases in the future. In order to understand this better, let me give you an example, suppose there is a call option with which you can buy option A for $120, but it is trading at $100, and there is another call option with which you can buy option A at $120, but it is trading at $140. Do you know which of these will have a greater value? It will be the second one because you are getting the chance to buy an option for a lesser price than what it is being traded for in the open market. Thus, the value of this option will be higher.
- **Strike Price** – The next factor that determines the price of an option is its strike price. The explanation is somewhat similar to that of stock price because it follows the same lines.

Before we discuss this further, you have to know how strikes are classified. There are three categories. 1) If the strike price is less than the stock price, then the call option is said to be in-the-money, 2) If the strike price is greater than the stock price, then the call option is said to be out-of-the-money, and 3) If the strike price is same as that of the stock price, then the call option is said to be at-the-money. If you consider the put option, then all of this will become exactly the opposite. The simple idea is that options will have a higher value when they are in-the-money than when they are out-of-the-money.

- **Option Type** – The type of option is also responsible for determining its value. Among all the other factors, this is probably the simplest one. As you already know that an option can either be a call or a put. The value will be determined based on the side of the trade or market you stand.
- **Time Left For Expiration** – Unlike stocks, options come with expiry dates, and so with time, their value is also affected. The value of an option will increase with an increase in the time left for expiration. But there will be a

decrease in the value of the option as the expiration date of your option comes closer. And when the option has reached the last 30 days of its life, that is when there is a rapid decrease in its value.
- **Interest Rates** – If we are speaking about the value of an option, then interest rates play a very small role. The value of a call option will rise with an increase in the interest rate, and the value of a put option will fall.
- **Dividends** – No dividends are received in the case of options, and so when dividends are released, you will notice a fluctuation in the price of the option. An ex-dividend date is set whenever dividends are released by a company. You will be getting that dividend if you still have the stock in hand on that particular date. Another thing to note is that, on the ex-dividend date, there will be a decrease in the value of the stock, and the decrease will be of the same amount as that of the dividend. With an increase in the value of dividends, there is an increase in the value of put options and a decrease in the value of call options.

- **Volatility** – The volatility factor is a big one when it comes to the price of options. The price of the stocks change every day, and this difference is referred to as the volatility. The strike price level of an option will keep changing with increased volatility. The factor of volatility that we are talking about here is called forward volatility, which, in simpler terms, means the volatility that is implied to be there in the future. People tend to predict a change in the price of a stock when the volatility increases. So, the price of options that have volatile stocks as their underlying assets has a higher price as compared to the ones that have non-volatile stocks. But you have to keep in mind that the factor of volatility that is being used here is more of an estimate.

How to Read Options Quote?

If you decide to trade options, one of the first things that you have to learn is how to read the quotes? Once you have chosen your broker, they will give you access to as many quotes as you want on a daily

Chapter 1: Important Concepts to Understand

basis, but if you don't know how to read them, you will not be able to proceed. The CBOE or Chicago Board Options Exchange is where you get information regarding the pricing of options, and you simply have to visit their section of Quotes and Data, which is present on their website.

If you go to the website, you will see that you can actually list the information by their expiration date. So, from there, you can basically select any month whose information you want to see. All you need to keep in mind that the month that you are selecting is actually the month of the expiry of an option. For example, if you are selecting Jan 20, then the expiration of that option is January 2020. The rest of the columns will show you information about the following – strike price, symbol, the price at which the last trade went through, the change in price, bid, ask, volume, open interest, and the Greek values.

Let me give you an example of a symbol so that you understand it better. If the symbol says SPY130524C00167000, then SPY stands for the stock symbol, 130524 is the year, month, and day – 2013,05,24, C stands for Call and 167000 is the strike price.

Chapter 2: Getting Into the Mindset of an Option Trader

Having the right mindset is so much important if you want to be a successful trader. It can actually be the game-changer. Like I already told you before, options are truly one of the most versatile instruments in the financial world. You simply have to learn how you can use them to your benefit, and one of the skills that you have to learn in the process is how you can acquire the mindset of an options trader.

Strategies to Think Like an Option Trader

Let me tell you about a little secret, which is not that much of a secret after all. If you truly want to become a successful trader, you should not only be excelling at figuring out the best strategies, but you should also be having a winning mindset. An extensive analysis can help you get your facts straight but when you are trading, your mindset can play a huge role. In fact, it is not the trading strategies or perfect market analysis or simple smartness that helps you win trades, but it is your psychological mindset that will get you a long way.

Chapter 2: Getting Into the Mindset of an Option Trader

Most of the beginners to whom I have interacted with have always told me the same thing – they are trying to figure out the right strategy, and they usually remain quite stressed about doing so. Most beginners think that once you have the best strategy, all you have to do is apply it and money will come rushing into your bank account. But that's not what happens.

Once you are in the trading world for quite some time, you will understand that trading is not all about strategies and numbers, and sometimes, it can even be tough. There are so many traders just like you who are waiting for their golden opportunity to become a millionaire, and they are all intelligent and well-learned. They even have designed full-proof strategies which are doubt solid. But you will notice that even they end up losing money from time to time.

On the other hand, there are traders who can show you a record of consistent wins, and do you know the secret behind their consistency? It is their psychological mindset. Trading psychology is actually a thing, believe it or not, and it is heavily researched too. There are several psychological characteristics, mindsets, attitudes, and beliefs that are studied under that system, and you have to know them too if you want to make it big in the trading world.

Some of the most common beliefs and attitudes about the market include you thinking that the market is actually rigged against you. But that is only a false belief that you have to breakthrough. It is erroneous and can put you in a negative state of mind. In fact, if you keep thinking like that, you won't be able to pull off your trades successfully. No one in the market is trying to go behind your back, and if you think so, then you simply have to change your perspective and look at it in a different way. If you continue to delve yourself in such baseless thoughts, then you will not be able to make a correct evaluation of the opportunities that arise in the market. Remember one thing very clearly – the market is not biased at all. In fact, it is totally neutral, and there is not a shred of doubt about that. The market does not care whether you are losing all your money or winning loads.

Your trading psychology is responsible for the beliefs that you have, and these beliefs can get so deeply rooted in your subconscious that sometimes they can

Chapter 2: Getting Into the Mindset of an Option Trader

push you into a toxic cycle of self-doubt. In the next section, we are going to discuss some of the characteristics an options trader should possess in order to be successful, and there, you will learn that confidence is, in fact, one of the most important qualities that you should possess.

If you analyze the mentalities of traders who have lost successively, you will notice that one thing is common with most of them, and that is — there is this nagging self-doubt that brings all the negativity in their life. You have to realize that you are actually walking on the path of a self-fulfilling prophecy if you think that you have bad luck and so you cannot win. You will have difficulty in initiating trades at the right time or implementing strategies at the right time if you doubt your abilities. You will not be able to take the call when you should. This can not only reduce your profits but can also create negative income.

On the other hand, winning traders don't think like that. They know how to respect the conditions of the market, and they know that sometimes, their strategies can mess up, or even if they did everything right, the trade can get messed up and they don't fall into an unnecessary cycle of self-blame. They are confident about themselves and the decisions they make. This confidence is the thing that separates them from losing traders, and they never miss a genuine opportunity coming towards them.

Another thing that is consistent with winning traders is that they know when a trade is losing them money and when it is simply a 'bad trade.' You might confuse them both to be the one and the same thing, but they are not. There is a critical difference, and I am going to explain that difference to you right now. Your trade cannot be classified as a bad trade just because you lost some money on it. That trade is basically a losing trade. The classification of a trade to be good or bad is not judged on the basis of whether you won it or lost it, but what matters is that when compared to the risk, the potential reward is more. Also, regardless of how the trade turns out to be, it will be a good trade if the probabilities or odds are in your favor. So, once you have taken a trade, if you are managing well with it no matter whether you win money or lose it, it will still be a good trade.

Similarly, if we are to think of the converse, even if you won money from trade, but the risk to reward ratio was bad, or if it was not initiated on good terms

Chapter 2: Getting Into the Mindset of an Option Trader

then no matter how much profit you made, that trade will still be considered to be bad.

Trading is quite a demanding task, and many people fail to understand that before jumping right into it. When you have a predetermined direction set in your mind, and the trade does not go your way, you will be facing a myriad of emotions, and the same applies to the scenario when the trade, does go in your direction. And thus, trades often face an adrenaline rush, which, in turn, leads to a threatening, dangerous, and stressful situation. No matter how calm and composed you are in your life, when you enter the trading floor, maintaining that same demeanor is quite a tough task. The stress and the pressure that you will be experiencing is something that you haven't before.

In order to truly think like an options trader, you have to learn how to think in probabilities. Yes, when it is your hard-earned money that is on the line, it might be a bit difficult to think in this way, but you simply have to learn it. Let us say that a particular strategy says that when applied to a bunch of trades, it will give you a 50-50 ratio of win/lose. So, even when you have this data in hand and have a full proof risk management strategy along with a trading plan in hand, what else can you do? Nothing, because you have to follow your trading plan.

In short, you should not be feeling too elated on a winning trade, neither too depressed on a losing one. This is because, in order to be a successful options trader, you have to realize that your trades are going to play out only 50% of the time and if you think about any one trade from the numerous trades you did, that one trade is only a small part of the grand scheme. It will definitely take you some time to develop this attitude and thinking, but you have to keep at it, and only then you will be able to develop the truckloads of discipline you need in order to be a successful options trader.

Important Traits of a Successful Options Trader

If you are wondering what traits of an options trader make him/her successful, then we are going to discuss that in this section. There is a reason that some traders can outperform others, and once you learn about these traits, I hope you will be trying to inculcate those in yourself.

Chapter 2: Getting Into the Mindset of an Option Trader

Ability to Manage Risk

You will probably hear everyone say this over and over again that proper risk management is what you need in order to be successful. And traders will not be able to use the risk management strategies if they are not accurate with risk assessment in the first place. Keeping in mind the factor of volatility, you have to understand what an explicit or implicit position is. You also have to assess what the major downside of trade can be. These are only a few questions that you should be asking yourself.

Once the risk is figured out, you have to able to find a way in order to mitigate the risk or control it. For example, if you are more into short-term trades in the world of options, there will be plenty of loss-making trades that you will come across in a day. Let us say, you decided to hold your position overnight, and on that same night, some adverse news was released, which completely changed the direction of the market, and so your bet goes bad. But your risk management strategy should be so good that it can control the risk no matter what the situation is. Diversification is just one of the strategies that traders use to minimize the risks involved in trade, and so their trade size is reduced.

Another trait that you should have in order to be a successful options trader is that you should be good at managing money. No matter how much capital you have, if you do not manage it wisely, it is ultimately going to go down the drain. One of the very common examples that I can give you is – suppose a trader used 90% of his capital on a single trade and the trade backfires, so he will end up losing almost all his money.

Have Discipline

Having proper discipline is going to get you far in your options trading career. But what does being disciplined means? It means that you have performed an ample amount of research, successfully identified the opportunities in the market that can work in your favor, set up the trade in the right way, form goals, use the right strategy, and also have an exit strategy. Do you know when you don't have discipline? It is when you don't practice anything of your own but simply follow the herd. Even if someone gives you a tip, you should not be trusting it

Chapter 2: Getting Into the Mindset of an Option Trader

until and unless you haven't performed your own research. When you incur a loss, it's on you and not on the person who gave you a tip because if you had performed your research, you would have identified what was wrong with the tip. That is why having an independent strategy is so important for everyone.

There are some traders who have completed an education in this field, but there are also so many successful traders who didn't study for options trading and are still making it big. So, it is totally your call whether you want to pursue your degree or not, but regardless of that, having a comprehensive idea about how the market works is important for everyone. If you simply do a Google search on 'how to make huge money in options trading' and think that you have learned everything, then you are wrong. You have to go into the details and learn everything that is there to know about the market and its workings.

Ability to Control Emotions

Controlling your emotions is a major part of trading psychology. Controlling your emotions doesn't only apply to times when everything is bad, but it also applies to the good times when you might have higher chances of making mistakes just because you are so excited about your win. If you ask most of the beginners in the market, they will all tell you the same thing; they had made more losses when they were excited and happy because of a win. No matter how many winning streaks you have, you have to stay grounded and not become over-confident.

In case any of your trades turn out to be wrong, you have to admit the fault and then back out. Don't ever let yourself get too attached to any particular stock; otherwise, it is going to ruin you. Stick to the rules you made in the beginning and don't divert from your path just because you are emotional.

Be an Active Learner

It has been said by the CBOT or the Chicago Board of Trade that out of everyone who is trading, 90% of them are going to witness losses. But the important thing here is to learn from the losses and mistakes that you have made instead of staying in denial about it. Practice and more practice is what is going to help you get ahead of others, and for that, you need to understand why those losses happened so that you can rectify your trade from the next trade onwards. The market is never stagnant and constantly keeps evolving. You have to evolve with it too, by being an active learner.

Keep a Record of Your Trades

The successful traders have the habit of recording their trades in a journal or anywhere. Do you know why? So that whenever a similar situation arises in the future, you remember what you did, and maybe you can apply the strategy again. All your trades that have been completed have a wealth of information only if you can recognize it and use it in your trades. This will put all the odds in your favor.

How to Determine the Right Time to Buy or Sell?

It is very important that you buy or sell your options at the right time; otherwise, you might not be able to bring home sufficient profits. So, here are some factors to keep in mind that will help you make your decision –

Is the Option Underpriced or Overpriced?

I know what you must be thinking – you are thinking how can you find it out whether an option is overpriced or underpriced. In order to find that, you simply have to calculate what its intrinsic value is. It is different from the way you do it in the case of equities, and the model followed in the case of options is called the Black & Scholes model. With this model, you will be able to find out the intrinsic value. I am not going into the details about the formula because once you go to your trading platform, you are going to get it there. What you need to understand here is that an option will be categorized as overpriced when its price is more than the intrinsic value, and such options have to be sold. On the contrary, an option will be categorized as underpriced if its price is less than the intrinsic value, and such an option has to be bough.

Check the Volatility

When you are trying to find out whether you should buy options or sell them, volatility plays a big role, and you are going to see how. Volatility is one such factor that can benefit both put and call options. On the upside, the option becomes much more valuable, and on the downside, there is limited risk. In simpler

Chapter 2: Getting Into the Mindset of an Option Trader

terms, if volatility increases, the value of an option increases too irrespective of the fact that the price of the stock is at the same point. So, when such an event occurs, you have to buy options and, on the contrary, sell the options when you notice a decrease in volatility.

Occurrence of Major Events

It is always advised that before any major events take place or before any geopolitical problem arises, you should not sell your options and rather buy them. Just imagine what would have happened if, before the Greek crisis, you had sold your put options. If you buy the options rather than selling, then all you will be losing is the premium paid. But if you choose to sell them, then there is a risk of your entire capital being wiped out.

Are You Taking a Defensive View or an Affirmative One?

Your decision to sell or buy an option will be greatly impacted by your view on the index or stock. Let me explain the meaning of both views so that we are clear. When you think that a particular stock is going to decisively go down or decisively go up, that is when you have an affirmative view. If your view is affirmative, depending upon the case, you can either buy a put option or a call option. But, on the other hand, if you have a defensive view, then you should be selling the option. For example, if you think that a particular stock A is not going to rise above $10, then it would be a better decision if you sell your $12 call option on this stock instead of buying.

Expiration Date

The expiration date or the time left to expiry is a very important factor of options that plays a role in almost everything. Like I already told you before, unlike stocks, there is a fixed date of expiry for every option contract before which it has to be exercised; otherwise, it will become useless. But this factor of time works in the favor of sellers and against buyers. The time decay is quite stable in the beginning, but as the time between now and the expiry date starts decreasing, the decay happens faster. In simpler terms, the value of the option decreases faster. So, when options are very close to their expiration date, it is not a good idea to buy them, is it?

It is a pivotal decision when it comes to whether you want to buy options or sell them, but whichever decision you make, you have to think it through.

Chapter 2: Getting Into the Mindset of an Option Trader

Chapter 3: Buying and Selling Call Options

In this chapter, we are going to discuss everything about call options and the long call strategy.

What Are Call Options?

A call option is a type of derivatives contract which gives the buyer the right to buy any financial instrument, including stocks at a particular price. This contract does not put you under any obligation. There is also a specified time within which you have to exercise the option. Another thing that you have to understand is that if you, as the buyer, decide that you want to exercise your option before the date of expiry at any particular time and make a purchase, then the seller is under an obligation to comply. The length of the expiration date can be anything starting from three days to a year. The purchase price of the option is given to the seller.

The purchase price is determined based on the proximity of the price of the underlying security to that of the strike price of the option at the time of purchase. It also depends on the time left until expiry

Chapter 3: Buying and Selling Call Options

because the time decay plays a role in this. In simpler terms, the price actually depends on the probability of a buyer being actually capable of exercising the option and also gain profits from it prior to the expiry date. If we consider the general scenario, then each option contract is composed of 100 shares.

If or when there is an increase in the price of the underlying asset to a level that is higher than the stock price of the option, then the call option buyer has a chance of making a profit. Alternatively, if or when the price of the underlying asset declines or never gets to go beyond the strike price of the option before the expiry date, then the seller of the call option makes a good profit. It is not advisable for a buyer to exercise their call option if the price of the underlying security has not gone beyond the strike price as expected. They simply have to leave the option as it is, and it will expire as an out-of-the-money option. The loss that you will incur as a buyer on this type of situation is the same as the price that you had paid to buy the call option in the first place.

So, when you are buying call options and if there is a rise in the price of the underlying asset, you get the chance of earning a profit or at least try to handle the positional risks by hedging.

Let me give you a clear idea of how the call options work. As you must already know, they are derivative instruments. So, the underlying asset of the call options is responsible for determining the price of the options.

For example, let us say the strike price of the call option XYZ is $100, and a buyer purchases them. The expiration date is that of 31st December. So, the buyer will then gain the right and not any obligation to get 100 shares of that company any time before the expiration date, which, in this case, is 31st December. Another thing that the buyer can do is that he/she can find another option buyer and sell the option before the expiry date. This transaction will be done at the contract's market price. Now, let us say that the value of the underlying asset declines, or even if it remains unchanged, then as the expiration date approached, the option value will start degrading.

Here are two purposes for which the call options are used by the investors –

Chapter 3: Buying and Selling Call Options

- **Speculation** – Like I already told you at the beginning of this chapter, the buyers of call options buy them because they speculate a price rise of the underlying security, and then they will be able to make some substantially good profits. By buying the option contract, they are paying only a meager amount of money when compared to the act of buying the stock shares on their own. The call options are a leveraged instrument, and so, with them, your chances of loss are limited, and yet your chances of profits are unlimited. But because of this leverage, the call options are also considered to be investments that involve a lot of risks.
- **Hedging** – The next purpose of the investors is to use the call options as hedging instruments. This is done by several institutions and investment banks. This prevents the losses of the investors because hedging is just like doing insurance so that even if an unforeseen circumstance arises, your risk has been minimized. In the case of short stock portfolios, it is these call options that are bought for hedging. In the case of

long stock portfolios, these call options are sold so that hedging can be done against a pullback.

What Is a Long Call Strategy?

Let us now discuss one of the most basic strategies that you will come across in options trading, that is — the long call strategy. In this type of strategy, you expect that the price of underlying assets of the call option that you just bought will increase and go beyond the strike price of the option. And this should happen before the options reach their expiration date.

So, in the case of a long call, there is a strike price A at which you get to buy the underlying asset of an option. If you are someone who doesn't want to go and buy stocks outright, then calls can be a good alternative for you. If the underlying asset increases in price, you will make a profit, and you do not even have to deal with all the risks that are associated with buying the underlying assets like stocks directly. But you also have to be careful with the long call strategy, especially with the out-of-the-money calls as they can expose you to greater risks. Read on to find out

Chapter 3: Buying and Selling Call Options

what the advantages of this strategy are and how you can make money with it.

Which Traders Use This Strategy?

This long call strategy is usually advised to veterans and those who are in higher ranks. Yes, there are beginners who start trading through short-term calls that are out-of-the-money only because they come cheap. They think that choosing such options is doing them good when, in reality, you are only posing a greater risk to yourself and your capital. This is not the right way of introducing yourself to the trading market.

Also, you should be using this strategy when the market is in a bullish condition because the speculation that traders have is that there will be a significant increase in the price of the underlying asset, and only then, they can make profits.

What Are the Advantages of This Strategy?

Before we move on to the list of advantages that this strategy, let us discuss some other factors that you need to understand.

Maximum Risk – The maximum risk in the case of this strategy is quite limited. In fact, it is going to be only that much amount of money that you paid for the call option. And this risk remains limited irrespective of the fact that the stock price is at its lowest on the date of expiration. If you want to calculate the maximum loss that you are going to incur, then you can do so by adding up the commissions that you have paid along with the premium. Also, this maximum loss will happen when the strike price of the long call is more than the price of the underlying asset.

Maximum Reward – The profit potential is unlimited in the case of the long call strategy. This is because, on the expiration date, the stock price can literally go as high as it wants, and there is no limit on that. So, when you are implementing the long call strategy, there is no limit on the profit that you can make from it. This maximum reward scenario is going to result when the strike price of the long call is less than the price of the underlying assets. Also, if you want to calculate the maximum reward that you can get, then you have to subtract the premium that you paid and

Chapter 3: Buying and Selling Call Options

the strike price of the long call from the price of the underlying asset.

Breakeven – The breakeven point refers to the strike price at which it is achieved, and you can find out the breakeven point for the long call strategy by adding the premium paid with the strike price of the long call.

Now, let's talk about the advantages that this strategy has –

- The first advantage is obviously the fact that the risk is limited, and at the same time, the potential for profit is unlimited, as explained above.
- The second one is related to the leverage in the case of the long call strategy. If you were to purchase the shares directly, the appreciation of value would not have been as fast as that happens when you purchase calls. Percentage-wise, the rise in the value of even the lower-priced calls is way more than the price of the underlying asset. In simpler terms, by opting for a long call strategy, you are getting more leverage than what you would have got by buying the underlying assets directly.

- You do not require much capital for the long call strategy as compared to the amount of money you would require to buy the underlying assets directly.

Now that you know the advantages, I think it is only just that you know about the potential disadvantages that can work against you –

- Time decay is probably the biggest enemy of this strategy. The option that you have bought will be negatively impacted with each passing day as you approach the expiration date.
- Another negative point is that if you make a wrong choice at any turn, you might lose the entire amount that you had invested in the option.

How to Effectively Use This Strategy to Generate Profits?

If you want to make profits by using this strategy, then the price of the stock has to move past the mark

Chapter 3: Buying and Selling Call Options

of – debit paid for the long call + option's strike price. After this mark has crossed, your profit potential does not have any limits. You can purchase the long call either out-of-the-money or in-the-money.

There are so many factors involved, and one of them is that you have to forecast the market correctly. There is a 2-part bullish forecast involved when you are buying the call. It goes on something like this –

- For the price of the call to increase, there has to be an increase in the price of the stock
- The rise in the price of the stock has to occur before the date of expiration

Now, let us discuss the strategy a bit more in detail. When you are speculating the price of a stock in order to buy the call, there are two decisions that have to be made, and the risk involved is limited. As you already know that the maximum risk that you have at this point is only the amount you paid to buy the call along with the commissions. In fact, you can reduce your loss, if you manage to sell the call at the right time way ahead of the expiration date.

So, do you know what your first decision is? It is deciding the right time to buy a call. When there is a decline in the stock price or even if it remains unchanged, the calls decline, and so you have to figure out the right time to buy it.

Now, coming to the second decision – you have to decide when is the right time to sell the call. This is because in case there is a change in the course of the stock price and it goes on a path of decline; then all your unrealized gains will disappear in a minute. Selling your call at the right time is what will help you bring your profits home.

There are so many investors who speculate that there will be an increase in price, and they have a target price set so that when that price is reached, or they estimate that the price will not be reached, they sell the call.

With every dollar change in the price of the underlying asset, the call price does not undergo the same change. The delta value plays a big role when it comes to these price changes. The delta value of calls that are at-the-money is usually 50%. Now, let us say there was a $1 fall or rise in the price of the

Chapter 3: Buying and Selling Call Options

underlying asset. The price of the at-the-money call will then undergo a fall or rise by 50 cents. On the other hand, the delta value of in-the-money calls is more than 50%, but they are never more than 100%. Similarly, in the case of out-of-the-money calls, you will get less than 50% delta values, but it will never dip below zero.

Here are some of the ways in which you can exit a long-call strategy –

- Close the positions at a profit by selling the options
- Sell the call while it is in-the-money and then you can use the money you get to buy a call that is out-of-the-money
- Exercise the call before the expiration date so that you own the stock
- Sell the call when it is out-of-the-money by going against the current position of the long call, and then you can create a spread
- The last way to exit is that you can let the option expire, and it will not have any worth then, but this process is not at all recommended.

An Example of the Long Call Strategy

Let us say that the price at which the stocks of an ABC company is trading is $40. Now, a call option contract that has its expiration date in a month has a strike price of $40, and the contract is priced at $2. You are speculating that there will be an increase in the price of stocks before the expiration date and so you buy a single ABC call contract of 100 shares at $200.

Now, let us look at the scenario where you were right, and there was an increase in the price. Suppose the price increases to $50 from $40. So, if you choose to exercise the option, you will be buying the 100 shares from the company ABC, and then you can sell the shares at the open market where they will be priced at $50 per share. So, with a profit of $10 for every share, you will be making $1000. Now, remember that you had used $200 for purchasing the call options, and so, now, your profit would be $800 ($1000-$200).

But in the scenario that you were wrong and the price of the stock reduced to $30 from $40, then you have to let your option expire, and it will become worthless, and so the loss that you will incur is $200

Chapter 3: Buying and Selling Call Options

— the amount that you initially paid to purchase the option.

Chapter 4: Buying and Selling Put Options

In this chapter, we are going to discuss everything about put options and the long put strategy.

What Are Put Options?

In the previous chapter, you learned about call options and how you can make a profit with them. No matter what kind of market we are talking about, for a buyer to exist, there has to be a seller too. In the same way, if we talk about the market of the options, if you don't have put options, you cannot have the call options either. But let us proceed to see what puts are.

These are basically contracts with which you will obtain the right to sell the underlying asset of that option before the expiration date at a specific price. But remember, just like the call option, here too, you are not under any obligation to do anything. The price at which you will sell the option is termed as the strike price. There are various underlying assets that can be traded as put options like commodities, currencies, and stocks. So, if you look closely, you will

Chapter 4: Buying and Selling Put Options

realize that the put options and the call options are exactly opposite to each other. But they still have some parts of them that are the same. In the case of the call options, there was a strike price and a predetermined date of expiration, just like the put options.

Here too, each contract of the puts will include a total of 100 shares of the underlying asset concerned. In order to sell or purchase puts, you don't have to actually own the asset. If you are the put option buyer, then you get the right to sell the asset within the expiration date at a particular price. Alternatively, if you are the put option seller, then you have the right and the obligation of buying the asset from the owner at the strike price if the owner has decided to exercise the option.

Whenever you buy a put option, your hope would be that there is a fall in the price of the underlying asset because only then you will be making money from put. You will learn more details in the latter part of this chapter. But you need to know this that put options are implemented in order to shield the money against a potential fall in the price of stocks, or they can also be used as nothing but speculative vehicles.

What Is a Long Put Strategy?

Just like the long call strategy, this is one of the basic strategies too. Here, you will be buying the put options when you have speculation that there will be a significant fall in the price of the underlying asset and that the price will go below the option's strike price. And this decline has to happen before the option approaches its expiration date.

If there is nothing like long puts and if the market moved down, then the only way in which you would have benefitted from it is by short-selling the stock. But do you know what the problem is with short selling stock? Well, you are exposed to a very high risk of an unlimited amount whenever there is a rise in the price of the stock.

But since you have puts, you get a better alternative rather than exposing yourself to an unlimited amount of risk. If you compare the long put strategy to that of short selling, you will understand that betting against a stock is much better than buy the put options. This is because you do not have to borrow anything. Moreover, the risk becomes limited. On the other hand, you have to keep in mind that there is a limited lifespan to the put options. If the movement in price does not happen before the option approaches its expiration date, your option will simply expire and be rendered worthless.

Which Traders Use This Strategy?

The long put strategy is also something that should be exercised only by those who are veterans or higher. What you have to look for in the market is a sharp decline in the price of the stock, and this has to happen before the expiration date of the option; otherwise, it would have no meaning to it. If you are trying to understand the compatibility, well, there are lots of forecasts in the long-term in which you can use this strategy. It can happen in neutral or even in bearish. But if you think that the outlook is firmly bullish, then you should consider looking at some of the other strategies which might be a better fit in such a situation.

What Are the Advantages of This Strategy?

Before we move on to the rewards or advantages linked to this strategy, there are certain things that you need to know in detail; otherwise, you won't be able to understand it.

Maximum Risk – The maximum risk involved is limited in the case of the long put strategy. It doesn't matter how much rise of stock price happens on the expiration date; the money that you can lose at its maximum is only the amount you paid for the premium. If you want to calculate the maximum amount of risk involved, you can do so by adding up the commissions that you have paid to the premium amount.

Maximum Reward – The long put strategy has unlimited potential for reward or profit from the trade. This is because, if we are to think theoretically, then the price of the stock can actually reach zero on the date of expiration. So, in simpler terms, the reward is limited to the strike price of the put that you bought, and you have to minus the option price from it.

Breakeven – Here the breakeven point is referred to the price at which it is achieved, and for this case, it is

Chapter 4: Buying and Selling Put Options

calculated by subtracting the premium paid from the strike price of the long put.

Now, let us talk about the advantages of the long put strategy —

- Firstly, as I have mentioned above, the risk is limited, and the potential for profit is unlimited.
- If you had to short the stock directly, it would have required you a much more amount of money than implementing a long put strategy in options.

I am also mentioning the disadvantages of this strategy because it is important that you know both —

- Time decay is an enemy in this strategy too, just like the long call strategy. With an increasing amount of time, the value of the option that you have bought will start decreasing at a progressive rate.
- Also, if you choose the expiration date or the strike price of the underlying asset wrong, you stand to lose every penny that you have invested in the option.

How to Effectively Use This Strategy to Generate Profits?

The long put strategy is specifically meant for the bearish market, and you have to use it when you think that in a fairly short amount of time, the price of an asset will go significantly down. But, you can use this strategy even if the drop in price is not going to happen in a short span but rather a longer span. In that case, one thing that you have to keep in mind is the effect of time decay. Puts have the characteristic of losing their intrinsic value over a certain period of time, and so when the drop in price happens over a longer time period, your profits will take a negative hit.

It is true that if you are expecting only a minor drop, then there are other strategies that can be used, but nonetheless, whenever there is a bearish outlook, you can use the long put strategy. Moreover, if your main aim is to protect one of your assets, the long put strategy can also be used as an effective hedging strategy.

The implementation of the long put strategy is not that difficult, and in fact, it is quite straightforward.

Chapter 4: Buying and Selling Put Options

You have to make only one transaction, and that is whatever security you are dealing with; you have to purchase the puts. In order to buy these contracts, you have to place a buy to open order through your broker.

When you are implementing this strategy, a total of three factors have to be taken under your consideration, and these are – the contract's expiration date, the option contract's strike price, and whether you want to purchase American style contracts or European ones. The answer will definitely depend on your preference as there is no hard and fast rule regarding any of them.

But two of the things that will be affected based on the strike price you select are – the potential profits you bring home from the trade and the price you pay. If you are starting out and do not have much experience of options trading, then I would suggest you stick to purchasing at-the-money contracts because, in their case, the underlying security's present trading price is equal to the strike price. In short, the at-the-money contracts will serve as a good middle ground for beginners. The alternative option to what I just said is that you can purchase out-of-the-money contracts, which will require paying a lower strike price, or if you purchase in-the-money contracts, then that will require you to pay a greater strike price.

If we consider from the price point of view, then the out-of-the-money contracts are definitely going to cost you less, but in order to make a profit with them, the price of the underlying asset will have to fall further down. And, they have to fall more than the at-the-money contracts. On the other hand, you will have to pay quite an amount for contracts that are in-the-money, but for them, the delta value is more. This means that if you compare them with the fall in the price of the underlying asset, the increase in value will be more rapid.

You have to figure out the time in which you think the underlying security will face the fall in price, and depending on that, you have to choose an expiration date. If your analysis says that the security is going to face a quick drop in price, then you should go for those contracts that are going to expire soon. Alternatively, if you think that the drop in price is going to happen over an extended period of time, then the better choice would be to go for contracts

Chapter 4: Buying and Selling Put Options

that still have time in hand before they reach their expiration date.

Now, let us talk about whether you should choose American style contracts or the European ones – well, honestly, the decision will depend on the amount of premium you are willing to pay. If you pay a higher premium, you will gain the advantage of exercise more flexibility on when you can exercise your option.

Like I told you before, you are going to profit from this strategy when there is a reduction in the value of the underlying asset. Your profit will increase with the decrease in the price of the security. In order to realize the profits you make from this kind of strategy – there are two ways, and I am going to talk about both here.

The price of the puts you own will increase with the decrease in the price of the underlying security. So, if you want, you can sell the puts at any time you want and make profits. This is what most traders do. But there is another way to reap the profits, and that is – you can choose to purchase the underlying asset, and then you can choose to sell it at the strike price. You will definitely incur more commission fees with this approach, and it is also a lot more complicated than what I advised you in the first instant.

If the price of the underlying asset is not able to fall below the price of the options you have or if it starts increasing, then you are going to lose money. But the worst thing that can happen while you are exercising this strategy is that the options that you have bought have expired worthless. And this would lead you to lose the entire money that you had invested in buying these options in the first place. So, if you think that the date of expiration of the options is coming close and there is no chance for the price to fall further, then you can take the approach of selling them so that you can at least recover a portion of the money you had invested initially.

An Example of the Long Put Strategy

Now, I am going to give you an example of this long put strategy to help you understand the whole thing better.

Let us say that the stocks of a company ABC is trading at a price of $50 and your prediction is that

Chapter 4: Buying and Selling Put Options

there will be a decrease in this price. For the stocks of this company, the price at which the at-the-money puts are being trades is $2. Suppose you invest an amount of $200, and you buy 1 contract for this put option (it will have 100 shares).

- If by the date of expiration, the price of the stock reduces to $48, then due to the intrinsic value of the puts, they will be of approximately $2 in value. So, if you manage to sell them at an amount of $200, you will successfully achieve the breakeven point.
- If by the date of expiration, the price of the stock reduces to $45, then the value of the puts at this point will be $5. In simpler terms, you will be able to sell them for an amount of $500. Since your investment was $200, your profit would be $300.
- If, by the date of expiration, the price of the stock is still at the level of $50 or increases from there, then the contract will become worthless at its expiration date, and you will lose the amount that you had initially invested, that is, $200. But I would like to mention something here that you are not actually obligated to let your options expire. If

you see that they are undergoing a price increase and you don't want to hold them all the way up till the end, then it's your call to sell them whenever you feel like it. In fact, if they show a decrease in price, you can sell them then too if you want to reduce your losses.

Chapter 4: Buying and Selling Put Options

Chapter 5: Covered Call Strategy

In this chapter, we are going to discuss another one of the very common strategies of options trading — covered call strategy.

What Is a Covered Call Strategy?

When an investor in the financial market owns a particular amount of underlying asset that is equivalent to the call options that he/she is selling, it is referred to as a covered call. In this type of strategy, the income generated comes in the form of premiums, and if your intention is that you want to keep the underlying stock with you for an extended period of time, then that is when you introduce this strategy.

You also should know that this is a neutral strategy. In simpler terms, if the life of the written call option is considered, then, as an investor, you can expect only a small decrease or increase in the price of the underlying stock. When the investor views the asset neutrally for the short term, they implement this strategy. So, they choose to hold the stock over the long-term since they cannot see any profits coming from it in the near future.

Chapter 5: Covered Call Strategy

You can view the covered call as a hedging strategy that lasts for a short-term on a long stock position. When you write the option, you receive a premium, and that is how you earn money from this strategy.

Which Traders Use This Strategy?

Covered calls are one such strategy that can be executed by any options trader irrespective of what level they are at. When you are writing a covered call, the simple explanation for this is that you are giving another person the right to purchase one of the stocks you own within a fixed time period. Since you are selling the call here, the premium will be in your account the moment you sell it. Another name that is used to refer to the covered calls is 'buy-write' mainly because the fundamental structure of this strategy states that it is a 2-part strategy where you first purchase the stocks, and then you move on to sell the calls on the basis of share-for-share.

What Are the Advantages of This Strategy?

The covered call strategy comes with three potential benefits, and we are going to discuss them in detail in this section.

- When you sell the covered call, you are receiving a premium, and you get to keep it as your income. In fact, there are several investors who will tell that the reason behind them using the covered call strategy in the first place is this. And, there are some investors who even have a program which helps them do this on a regular basis – in some cases quarterly and in others, monthly. Their only goal from all this is that their annual returns can increase by adding this extra cash income, and they are definitely going to make a difference by several percentage points.
- As an investor, when you sell covered calls, it becomes easier for you to aim for a selling price that is more than the current price of the stock. Let me give you a simple example – let's say you have bought a stock which was $39.30 for each share. For 0.90 per share, a 40 Call is sold. Now you will have to sell the stock when the covered call is assigned, then you receive $40.90, and this does not take

the commissions into account. Let us say that the stock does not rise much and stops at $40.50, assigning the covered call would mean, you receive $40.90. Now, with the help of the covered call, you can target this objective, and the only thing required is that the investor should be willing to sell it at this price level, and you will be making money even when the price of the stock does not reach that level.

- The third major benefit of following this strategy is the downside protection that the investors get. If we are to carry on with the example that I just stated in the previous section, the risk is reduced because the breakeven point is reduced because of the $0.90 premium per share. But do not forget that the protection is quite small and limited because the premium is only a small percentage of the total stock price.

How to Effectively Use This Strategy to Generate Profits?

Start by selecting a stock after going through your portfolio thoroughly. The stock that you choose should be the one that has already shown good results in the past, and in case the call option is assigned, you should be willing to sell the stock. If there is a stock that, in the long-term, you are very bullish about, steer clear of such stocks because this will prevent you from being too sad about losing the stock.

Now, it's time to pick a strike price. What I would advise you is that settle for an out-of-the-money strike price because your ultimate aim with this strategy is that the price should rise before you sell it.

The next step is choosing the date of expiration. You have to put your judgment to good use, but for the starting point, I would say something like 30-45 days should be good. The date should be reasonable enough with respect to the strike price you have chosen and also gives you a good premium after you sell it.

The norm is that an acceptable premium amount should be 2% of the value of the stock. Never forget that you are trading options, and in the case of options trading, the real money lies with time. The value of an option will be more, the further you

Chapter 5: Covered Call Strategy

decide to go in time. But it might become tougher to give a correct prediction as you move forward into the future. Now, let us look at the outcomes that you might arrive at from this –

The Price of the Stock Decreases

The good news with the fact that the price of the stock has decreased is that when the expiration date comes, the stock will expire without having any value. The premium for selling the stock will be in your hands. But the downside is that the value has reduced, but that is what a covered call is all about.

Let us say that the price of the stock decreased way before the expiration date. In that case, whatever you do, don't start panicking. You have to remember that you are not locked or obliged to be where you are. With a decrease in price, the losses are accumulating, but with a decrease in value of the call option you sold, the greater will be your possibility of purchasing it back for lesser than what you had to sell it for. In case you are no longer of the same opinion on the stock, you can choose to dump it by simply buying the call contract back, and your position will be closed.

The Price of the Stock Increases a Bit or Stays the Same But Does Not Touch the Strike Price

If this situation happens, it is not really bad news because the call option you decided to sell with reach its expiration date, and it will become worthless, and so, when you sell it, you get to keep the whole premium. You might even realize some profits from the underlying asset because it still belongs to you.

The Price of the Stock Increases and Goes Beyond the Strike Price

Let us assume a scenario where at the expiration date, the price of the stock is more than its strike price. In that case, you are required to sell the 100 shares of the stock because the call option will be assigned.

Now, after the shares have been sold, there might be a situation where the stock starts skyrocketing, and I am sure you will start blaming yourself for missing out on potential gains but don't. You have to remind yourself that you actually brought home maximum profits that were possible through the covered call strategy, and for that, you intentionally made a decision, which was the right decision at the time. Just

Chapter 5: Covered Call Strategy

appreciate exercising patience and presence of mind because you have done it well.

An Example of This Strategy

Let us assume that you own the shares of a Company X. You think that the long-term prospect of the company is good, and you also love the share price, but you think that the stock will probably not witness any growth in the short-term. Currently, the price of the stock is $25.

If you select a strike price of $27 and sell a call option on Company X, then from this sale, you will earn a premium, but the upside of the stock will be capped to $27 during the term of the option. If for the 3-month call option, the premium received is $0.75, then it will amount to $75 for each contract since each contract has 100 shares.

In such a situation, either one of the following two scenarios is going to play out –
- The shares are trading at a price below the strike price of $27. In that case, the investor will get the premium, and on the date of expiration, the option will expire, and it will no longer have any value. So, the stock will be

outperformed by the implementation of the buy-write strategy. The investor will still be in possession of the stocks but at the same time, have an amount of $75 in his/her pocket.

- In the second scenario, we are going to see what would happen if the price goes above $27. The upside of this is that the price of the stock will be capped at $27, and the option will be exercised. Now, if we add the premium to the strike price, it becomes $27.75, and if the stock trades at a price more than this, then it would be advisable that the investor holds on to the stock. But if the investor still thinks that he/she should sell the stock at $27, then they will get an extra amount of $0.75 for each share by writing the call option.

What Is the Risk/Reward In This Strategy?

When you are holding the position of the stock in a covered call, that is when you have to deal with the risk because the price may drop at any time. If the price of the stock goes down to zero, that is when you incur the maximum loss. So, the calculation for the maximum loss for each share should be something

Chapter 5: Covered Call Strategy

like this = Entry Price of Stock – Premium of Option Received

Let us consider that you receive a premium of $0.10 for a stock that is $9 in price on a call that you sold. So, your maximum loss here would be $8.90 for each share. Your maximum loss is reduced by the amount of money from the premium. But at the same time, the upside of the stock is lowered.

The profit is capped to the strike price of the options sold, and hence, the profit potential is not unlimited. So, the maximum profit that you can make with this strategy is –
(Strike Price of the stock – Entry Price of the stock) + Premium received on the option

Here is an example – if you receive a premium of $0.10 after buying a stock at $9 and selling it at $9.50, then the position of your stock will be maintained as long as the price does not cross $9.50 before the expiration date. But if suppose the price moves to $10, then the profit that you will make will be capped to $9.50 which is calculated as $9.50-$9 +$0.10 = $0.60

When you are following the covered call strategy, don't forget to factor in the commissions. If the commissions are so huge that they are going to negate your premiums, then you should reconsider whether creating a covered call would be a worthwhile option in the first place.

Chapter 6: Protective Put Strategy

Chapter 6: Protective Put Strategy

In this chapter, we are going to learn about the protective put strategy, which is basically a type of hedging strategy in options trading.

What Is a Protective Put Strategy?

Both traders and investors face a common challenge when it comes to options, and that is risk vs. reward. This is the reason why we need hedging tools, and the protective put strategy is one such hedging tool. In this strategy, you aim to protect yourself from a drop in the price of the underlying security by buying that put. This strategy is applied when the trader is still in a bullish environment with respect to a stock that he/she owns, but they know that in the near future, some hurdles might appear on the path. The main of this strategy is to protect those gains of a previous purchase that are still unrealized. In simpler terms, it is a risk management strategy. This strategy can be used in the case of currencies, stocks, indexes, and even commodities. In the unfortunate event that the price of the underlying asset declines, the protective put is what will serve as your insurance policy.

Chapter 6: Protective Put Strategy

Sometimes, you will notice that the term synthetic long call is being used to refer to protective put. Do you know why? Well, it is because the loss and profit potential in the case of a protective put are quite similar to that of a basic call option.

The strategy is created by owning or buying assets and purchasing put options on the basis of share-for-share. Let us say you owned or purchased 100 shares, and you have also bought one put. In case there is a decline in stock price, you don't have to worry because below the strike price, you will get protection with the purchased put. But there is something that you need to remember – the protection offered by the put is only until the stock reaches its expiration date. If there is an increase in the price of the stock, then you will be participating fully, excluding the cost of the put.

Which Traders Use This Strategy?

Investors who made a purchase and still own the shares of that previous purchase with unrealized profits (which accumulated when the value of those shares increased) are the ones who use this strategy. They use this when they think that the market might be at risk in the near future and so they are seeking some kind of protection for their unrealized profits. So, they implement this directional strategy where they buy puts while still having the shares of the underlying stock from the previous purchase. Both rookies and higher-ups can use this strategy, especially when they are bullish but are nervous about it.

What Are the Advantages of This Strategy?

Now, we are going to discuss the different advantages linked with this strategy –

Unlimited Potential for Profit

On using this strategy, the potential for profit is unlimited. In simpler terms, the maximum profit that is attainable with this strategy is unlimited. You can find it out by subtracting the premium paid and the purchase price of the underlying asset from the current price of the underlying asset.

Limited Risk

The maximum loss that a trader or investor can incur after implementing this strategy is limited, and the loss would be equal to the premium that you had paid at the time of purchasing the put option.

So, the maximum loss can be found out by this formula –
Premium + Underlying Asset's purchase price – Strike Price of put option + Commissions

How to Effectively Use This Strategy to Generate Profits?

There is a two-part forecast that a trader has to master in order to generate profits with the protective put. The first thing is that the forecast must be bullish. You have to remember that you are holding or buying the stock because it is bullish. The second part of the strategy is to find ways in which you can limit your risk exposure. For example, the stock price can move with a sharp magnitude in either direction if there is a pending earnings report. If we assume such a situation is about to happen and if the report turns out to be positive, then your position will remain protected when you buy a put, and at the same time, the risk towards having a negative report is considerably reduced.

Another situation is if you think there will be a reverse upward motion in a downward trending stock, then your risk of the prediction not becoming true will be limited when you buy a put.

There are 1 disadvantage and 2 advantages associated with following the strategy of buying a put as I mentioned above. For starters, your exposure to risk will be limited as long as the put is valid, and the second advantage is that following this strategy is different from that of placing a stop-loss order. Whenever there is some random sharp fluctuation in the price, the stop loss has a chance of getting triggered because of its price-sensitive nature, but that does not happen with a protective put because it is not limited by the price but by time. On the other hand, the disadvantage is that the cost of the put will be added to the total stock's cost.

When the stock reaches expiration, if the strike price is above the stock price, then you have to make a choice among these two options –

- You can choose to keep the stock position unprotected by selling the put

Chapter 6: Protective Put Strategy

- You can extend the protection on your stock position by selling the put and then buying another put
- Lastly, you can choose to exercise the put, which means you will be selling the stock. After that, you can invest the money somewhere else.

Now, none of the choices that I mentioned above are right or wrong. You simply have to decide what is best for you. Thus, it is completely a personal decision.

Now, I am going to briefly discuss the impact of a change in the stock price. When you add the put price with the stock price, you get the total value of the protective put position. If there is a rise in the underlying stock's price, the total value also increases. Alternatively, when the underlying stock's price falls, the total value decreases. There is another thing that you should know, and that is – how volatility can impact the protective put. The fluctuation of the prices of stocks is what volatility signifies, and prices of options are influenced by the concept of volatility. Let us consider that the expiration period and stock price remains constant, then the price of options tend to rise with a rise in the volatility of the underlying asset. So, in the case of a long put, rising volatility is considered to be a good thing, and falling volatility is considered to be a bad thing. This, in turn, means that with an increase in volatility, the protective put value will increase, and it will fall, when volatility decreases.

You can basically buy the contract of a protective put any time you want, but some people prefer buying them at the time of stock purchase. But if you want, you can even purchase them at a later date. As you must have already understood, with the help of the protective put, you can maintain unlimited potential gains and limited losses. But the long stock position will benefit when the price of the stock keeps rising, and then the put option that you bought will no longer be needed and will expire worthlessly. In such a case, all that you lose will be limited to the premium that you had initially paid. In case the original put expires worthlessly, the trader or investor can choose to invest in another protective put.

The protective puts can either shield the entire holdings of the investor or only their long position. But there is a separate strategy called the married put when the long stock amount is equal to the ratio of

Chapter 6: Protective Put Strategy

coverage offered by the protective put. You will learn about married puts in Chapter 9.

An Example of This Strategy

Let us assume that an investor has bought 100 shares of a company X where the price of each share was $10. Now, if there is an increase in the price of the stock to suppose $20, then the investor will have unrealized gains of $10 per share because they haven't yet been sold.

If the investor thinks that the price might increase a bit more in the near future, then he/she might not be willing to sell the stock, but at the same time, they do not want to suffer a loss of $10 per share, which is unrealized. So, that is when the investor can make a choice of purchasing a put option so that as long as the contract is valid, a portion of the profit will remain protected.

Let us say; a put option is purchased by the investor at $15 for 75 cents as the strike price. So, even if we are to consider the worst situation, then the stock will have to be sold for $15. The expiration date of the stock is approaching in the next three months, and if during that time, there is a fall in the price of the put to $10 or even lower, then there will be a dollar-for-dollar profit for the investor.

As you know, the premium cost of the option is $75 (100 shares x $0.75), so the minimum profit that the investor has locked is $425 because Strike Price ($15) – Purchase Price ($10) = $5 – Premium ($0.75) = $4.25 x No. of shares (100) = $425.

On the other hand, the investor would not have any profit if the put option is not bought, and the price of the stock decreases to $10. But when the put is purchased and if the price increases, as predicted, to say $30, then the investor will make a profit of $20 per share. When multiplied with 100 shares, it gives the investor a total profit of $2,000. From this, you have to deduct the premium paid that is $75, so the net profit will be $1,925. But yes, you have to deduct the commissions paid as well or any other charges that you had to pay during the trade.

What Is the Risk/Reward In This Strategy?

As already explained in the above sections, the risk is limited, and the profit potential is unlimited in the

Chapter 6: Protective Put Strategy

case of this strategy. The protective put is basically considered to be a hedging strategy because it helps in minimizing the risks of investors. So, anyone looking forward to a strategy to mitigate huge losses, this strategy can be your friend. The maximum loss that you can incur while exercising this strategy is limited and equal to the price you paid for purchasing the underlying asset and also add the commissions to this and subtract the put option's strike price. So, simply framed, the underlying asset's losses come to a stop at the strike price of the option.

The ideal situation for anyone using the protective put strategy is that there will be a significant increase in the price of the put because the long stock position is going to be beneficial for the investor.

Also, something that has not been mentioned in the previous sections is that when you are using this strategy, there are certain important tax considerations to keep in mind. The holding period of the stock is directly affected by the timing of the protective put. So, the rate of taxes applicable to both losses and profits is affected.

Chapter 7: Straddle Strategy

Now, let us move on to another new strategy called the straddle strategy, and we are going to cover everything in detail about this strategy. It is basically a neutral strategy.

What Is a Straddle Strategy?

In the case of a straddle strategy, the trader is purchasing both calls and put options at the same strike price for the underlying asset, and the date of expiration is also the same for both of them. When the price of the stock either falls or rises by an amount that is equivalent to the total premium you paid, you make a profit.

If we are speaking more broadly, then I would say that there are a total of two transactions involved when we are discussing the straddle strategy. And both the transactions are related to the same underlying asset, and the component transactions balance each other. Whenever the trader predicts that the price of the stock might witness a significant movement, but they are not sure about the direction of movement, they implement the straddle strategy. There are two things that you can learn about the

Chapter 7: Straddle Strategy

market from the straddle strategy. The first thing is the amount of volatility for the underlying asset that the market is anticipating, and the second thing is the trading range of the underlying asset before the date of expiration.

There are several sophisticated neutral strategies that you will come across in options trading, and they are used in situations when the trader is not sure about the direction of price movement, but compared to all other strategies, the straddle is a relatively easier and less complex one. The main aim is to enable the trader to make a profit irrespective of the direction of price movement. There are two types of straddle strategies – one of them is the long straddle, and the second one is the short straddle, and in this chapter, we are going to discuss how you can use the long straddle to your own benefit.

What Is the Long Straddle Strategy?

The put and the call that is purchased in the case of a straddle strategy has the same expiration date and strike price. The increasing volatility is exploited in the case of a long straddle strategy. When the price of the underlying asset goes below the lower breakeven point or rises above the upper breakeven point, that is when this strategy will give you profits. The strike price, in this case, is either at-the-money or at least as close to it as possible. Now, as you might already know that when there is a downward move in price, it is the puts that benefit from it and when there is an upward move in price, it is the calls that benefit from it. Since this strategy involves both, so all the small moves in either direction are canceled out, so a profit is made whenever there is a strong move in either direction. Such moves can be triggered by an important announcement or news.

When you think that there is going to be the release of an earnings report, an election, or any such major event, you can implement the long straddle. The traders, in this case, are basically waiting for such an event to happen so that they can make profits. The pent up bearishness or bullishness is released during the event, and there is a quick and sudden movement in the price of the underlying stock. The result of the event is not known, and so the trader is also not aware of whether they should be bearish or bullish. So, the only logical solution in such a scenario is the use of the straddle strategy so that no matter what the outcome is, you can still make a profit from

Chapter 7: Straddle Strategy

it. But even this strategy has its own challenges, just like any other strategy.

The main risk associated with this strategy is that even if there is a news or event that is going to take place, it might not make the market react strongly enough. The effect is even more compounded because the impending event is common knowledge and thus leads to an increase in the price of both call and put options. So, if you compare the strategy with that of betting in any one direction, this is much costlier to attempt. In fact, if no major news event happens in the near future, then the cost of approaching the straddle strategy is way costlier than betting in both directions.

Now, the risk associated with any event that is worthy of news is realized by the option sellers too, and so they raise the prices so that about 70% of the predicted event can be covered. So, this acts as a drawback, and the profit-making chances are reduced because small changes in either direction are already included in the straddle. So, in case there is no strong change after the probable event, then the trader is most likely to incur a loss because the option contract will expire worthlessly.

Which Traders Use This Strategy?

Only seasoned veterans and higher-ups should be using this strategy because it is not a strategy for beginners. In fact, at first glance, it is very easy for you to think that it is easy to execute, but not all investors are suited for this. Your forecasting ability should be really great and advanced in order for you to benefit from this strategy. As already mentioned in the above section, the implementation of the straddle strategy should be done when you are anticipating the stock price to undergo a strong change, but you are unsure about the direction of the change. Thus, the stock can either go down the drain, or it can shoot right through the roof.

What Are the Advantages of This Strategy?

Now, let us have a look at some of the major advantages that this strategy has to provide you.

- The first advantage is definitely the unlimited profit potential because there is no bar as to how high the price of the stock can rise. Also, since both puts and calls are involved, no matter which direction the price of the stock

Chapter 7: Straddle Strategy

takes, there is a chance of a substantial amount of profit in both cases as long as the change is strong. Moreover, even if there is a decrease in the price of the stock, the profit might still be substantial, but it will be limited to the strike price after subtracting the net debit you paid.

- No matter how volatile the stocks are, you can put them to good use and make a substantial amount of profits without even finding out which direction they are going to move.
- The risk exposure is quite limited in the case of these stocks because the maximum loss is equal to the total cost of the straddle along with the commissions you paid. In such a scenario, both your options will expire worthlessly.

But since the strategy has some significant disadvantages too, I think it is crucial you know them as well.

- One of the major disadvantages is the factor of time decay, and it becomes the mortal enemy. Both the options, that is, the put option as well as the call option, will decrease

in value as time goes by, and so the factor of time decay is double for this strategy. That is why it is crucial that you make the right choice regarding the expiration date, strike price, and the underlying stock.
- Also, in order to make the strategy profitable, a significant movement in price is required no matter what the direction is.

How to Effectively Use This Strategy to Generate Profits?

Out of all the volatility strategies, the long straddle is the most popular and easiest one. The main idea behind the strategy is that you need to purchase the same number of calls and puts at the same expiration date and strike price and you will incur a profit irrespective of the direction of price movement. So, the only thing that you have to care about is that the stock moves in any one direction by a sharp number. You don't really have to worry about the direction as long as the movement is sharp.

In order to ensure that this strategy is profitable, the value of the call options should increase, and this should be more than the decrease in the value of put

Chapter 7: Straddle Strategy

options. On the contrary, there is another situation in which you can make a profit, and that is when the increase in the value of the put options is more than the fall in the value of call options. No matter what the strike price is when the stock is at-the-money, this strategy can be executed. But there is another thing that you should try to ensure – the implied volatility should be low. Low implied volatility means that the price of the option will be low, but there is a probability for an explosive move in one of the directions. Keep in mind that since you are paying the premium for the call options as well the as the puts options, this is a net debit trade.

An Example of This Strategy

Like I mentioned in the previous section, there are limited risk and unlimited profit potential in the case of the straddle strategy. If there is an increase in the underlying asset's price, the chances of making a profit are unlimited. The profit would become limited to the strike price minus the premiums you paid if the underlying asset's price becomes zero. But no matter whichever scenario you face, the total risk is always going to be capped at the total cost that you had to bear in order to enter this position in the first place.

Here is an example to make the concept clearer to you.

Suppose the price of each share of a stock is $50, and an investor implements the straddle strategy by purchasing a call option and a put option, both of which have their strike prices at $3. This means that the trader thinks that there is more than a 70% chance of the price of the stock becoming $6 or less than that in either direction. But irrespective of what the initial price was, the trader's position will bring him profits is the price of the stock is either below $44 or above $56 at the time of expiration.

The maximum loss that a trader can incur is $6 per share, and it will happen only when the price of the stock is at $50 and no more or no less on the day of expiration. But if the price is something else between $44 and $56, then the amount of loss incurred will be less. But anything more than those values is going to bring the trader profits. Let us say that the price of the stock becomes $66 on the day of expiration, then the profit from that position would be $10 ($66-$56).

What Is the Risk/Reward In This Strategy?

Chapter 7: Straddle Strategy

The maximum risk that you can incur with this strategy is limited to the total premium that was paid for the at-the-money puts and calls. On the other hand, the maximum reward is unlimited because there is no limit to the downward or upward movement of the stock.

There are three ways in which you can exit a trade where you applied the straddle strategy, and they are –

- If there is a surge in the price of the underlying asset in the upward direction, then you can sell the call options, and in order to profit from the put options, you can wait for the pullback.
- In case the price of the underlying asset drops down, then you can sell all the put options, and then in order to profit from the call options, you have to wait for the retracement.
- You can sell both the calls and puts, and this will offset your position.

Chapter 8: Strangle Strategy

Just like the straddle, the strangle strategy will also help you to benefit from the trade no matter what the direction of price movement is. Here too, you are going to buy put, and call options of an equal amount, and both of them should have the same expiration date. The only difference between strangle and straddle is that in the case of the straddle strategy, the strike prices of both the options were the same whereas, in the case of strangle, the strike prices are different.

What Is a Strangle Strategy?

To put it in simpler terms, there is no directional bias associated with the straddle strategy, but in the case of a strangle, the trader has a belief that there will be movement in a certain direction or at least there is a greater chance for the stock to move in that direction, but even then, the trader wants to protect his position in the event that there is a negative move.

What Is a Long Strangle Strategy?

Chapter 8: Strangle Strategy

Now there are two types of strangle strategies – one of them is the long strangle, and the other one is the short strangle. In this chapter, we are going to discuss the long strangle in even more detail. The main aim of the long strangle is to help you make a profit whenever the stock undergoes a huge change in price in either direction.

This strategy is comprised of one long put that has a lower strike price and a long call that has a greater strike price. The expiration dates of the underlying assets of these options are the same, whereas the strike prices are different. This type of strategy is based on net debit, and it will be profitable if the price of the underlying stock decreases and goes below the lower breakeven point or goes above the upper breakeven point. On the upside, the potential for making profits with this strategy is unlimited, and on the downside, it is substantial. On the other hand, the potential loss in this type of strategy is capped by the total cost of the strangle and any commissions that you had to pay.

You are going to incur a loss with this strategy if you trade less volatile stocks because for the stock price to move beyond the put or the call, there has to be high volatility.

Which Traders Use This Strategy?

Just like the straddle, only seasoned veterans and higher-ups should approach using this strategy because it might seem fairly simple to you in the beginning, but executing it in the right way is not everyone's cup of tea. Your forecasting ability should be really sharp and advanced for you to profit from this strategy. Traders usually implement this strategy when they think that there is going to be an abnormally huge move in the stock price because of a major event or news. For example, if an earnings announcement is approaching, then you can consider running this strategy prior to that. But unless and until you are dead certain about that huge swing in price, I think you should stick to long straddle instead of long strangle. I know that it is costlier to run a straddle, but the breakeven points are closer than that of the strangle, and so the stock can outrun those points even when the move is not that huge.

What Are the Advantages of This Strategy?

Chapter 8: Strangle Strategy

Now, let us look at some of the advantages that this strategy has to provide you —

- The first advantage of the long strangle is that it is less expensive as compared to the long straddle. Now, this strategy deals with options that are out-of-the-money, which you already know have a lower premium as compared with the options that are at-the-money.
- The second advantage is that the maximum loss that a trader can incur with this strategy is limited. This maximum loss situation happens when at the time of expiration, the price of the underlying stock is trading in a range that is between the strike price of the call option and the put option that you just bought. In such a scenario, the options will reach their expiration, and they will expire worthlessly. The initial debit that you had to pay in order to enter the trade will be lost.
- The potential for profit in this strategy is unlimited, and that is one of the biggest advantages too. This happens when there is a huge move in the price of the underlying stock so that it crosses and goes beyond the strike price of either option.

There is only one disadvantage associated with this strategy, and that is – in order to make a profit from this strategy, the movement has to be quite huge. But you should also consider time decay because with time, both the options lose their value, and the factor of time decay is double because of the involvement of both call and put options.

How to Effectively Use This Strategy to Generate Profits?

You have already learned about the long straddle strategy in the previous chapter. This strategy is quite similar to that with just one difference because a slight adjustment has been made to make this strategy cost-effective. In order to ensure that you bring home profits from this strategy, the increase in the value of the call options has to be more than the decrease in the value of the put options. Or, you can also make a profit when the increase in the value of the put options is more than the decrease in the value of the call options. The strike prices that you choose for this strategy can be of any desired combination, but usually, it is established near an at-

Chapter 8: Strangle Strategy

the-money option towards the mid-point of the strike price.

Another thing that you should ensure is that the stock has low implied volatility so that the price of the options is low, but there should be a probability for the stock to make an explosive move in a direction. If you consider from your intuitive point of view, you will realize that implanting the strangle strategy is really a very lucrative option because you are going to make a profit irrespective of the direction of movement of the stock. But both of your selling and buying decisions have to be perfectly timed in order to truly benefit from this strategy.

In simpler terms, volatility expansion is one of the main things on which the success of the strangle strategy depends. The sharp price movement can be brought about by anything like earnings reports, important announcements, or even the verdict of a lawsuit. In some cases, the traders prefer to take the benefit of a low volatility situation and purchase the strangle at that time so that when after the announcement, the volatility increases, they can sell the option and make a huge profit.

But you have to decide whether you have to implement a long straddle or a long strangle, and the decision will have to be made after judging the probability of the stock to make a huge movement and the amount of the cost that you want to bear.

An Example of This Strategy

Let us say that in June, a particular ABC stock is trading at $40. A long strangle is executed by the options trader, and so with $100, he purchases a JUL 35 put and for another $100, a JUL 45 call. So, for entering the trade, the total amount paid was $200, and this is also the amount of loss that the trader can incur at a maximum level.

Let us assume that the stock rallies and at the time of expiration, it is trading at $50; in such a case, the call will expire in-the-money whereas the put will expire worthlessly and the total intrinsic value will be $500. If we minus the total cost of entering the trade, that is $200, then the net profit for the trader is $300.

If the stock is still trading at $40 at the time of expiration, then both the options are going to expire worthlessly, and the total loss that the trader will

Chapter 8: Strangle Strategy

have to suffer is equal to the initial debit, that is, $200.

What Is the Risk/Reward In This Strategy?

The maximum risk is the net debit invested at the beginning of the strategy, and the maximum reward is basically unlimited because the underlying stock can show downward or upward movement without any limits. The upside breakeven is calculated by adding the net premium paid with the strike price. The downside breakeven is calculated by subtracting the net premium paid from the strike price.

Chapter 9: Bonus Strategies Explained

We have already spoken at length about the common strategies of options trading. In this chapter, we are going to see some other strategies in detail, and I will also tell you when the best time to apply them is.

LEAPS

The first strategy that we are going to learn about is LEAPS, which is an acronym for long-term equity anticipation securities. It is advised that you use this strategy, especially when you are in bullish conditions, with respect to the stock of a particular company. In fact, this strategy can give you a 300% gain simply with a 50% rise. So, let us see how it works.

What Are Leaps?

If you are inclined towards investing in options for the long-term, then LEAPS are what you should be looking at. These are basically exchange-traded options where you can get an expiration date to as much as three years. In the case of standard options,

Chapter 9: Bonus Strategies Explained

the expiration date falls on a monthly basis, but with LEAPS, you can not only invest in a broader market but also hedge or find different ways to trade the options. If you had purchased the stock direction, then you would have ended up buying way more than the amount of money you are going to invest in these options. All you have to do is figure out the direction of movement right, and you are in for some outsized returns.

Buying Stocks vs. LEAPS

Some people are still concerned about the fact that why should they invest in LEAPS in the first place. So, I am going to show you a comparison between LEAPS and stocks.

Let us say that you are interested in the stocks of Company ABC, and you want to buy multiple shares that are trading at a price of $14.50 per share. Now, you have a total capital of $14500 available for investment. You have performed sufficient analysis, and you think that the price of the shares is going to rise in the upcoming years, and the rise is going to be substantially high. So, if you want to invest in the stocks of this company, there are three options open in front of you. You can buy the stocks on margin, buy then outright, or invest in LEAPS.

Before we move into further discussion, I just want to let you know the meaning of the term 'buying on margin.' It means that in order to buy the shares, you are borrowing money from the broker, and it is nothing but a loan. The collateral is in the form of the shares you purchased. If your prediction turns out to be wrong, then you will lose a huge chunk of money, and it will be more than the invested amount.

Now, coming back to our discussion — we are first going to see what happens when you decide to purchase the stocks on margin or outright. The simple mathematics would tell you that with a capital of $14,500, you can purchase 1000 shares. Or, if you are buying or margin with a leverage of 2 to 1, then you can buy 2000 shares with an investment of $29,000, but in that case, you will incur a debt of $14,500. But if the stock crashes or something wrong happens, you will have to sell at a loss. And if you had borrowed the money, you will not only have to pay the original amount back but also pay it back with interest.

Chapter 9: Bonus Strategies Explained

So, what happens if you choose the approach that involves LEAPS? If you check the pricing tables, you will find that you can purchase the stocks of Company ABC by purchasing a call option that has its strike price at $17.50. The expiration date might be two years. Now, you already know that options are contracts, and they have 100 shares within each. So, if you buy 100 contracts with $14,500, you will actually be exposed to 10,000 shares. Let us assume that for each share, the premium paid is $1.50, so the total premium would be $15,000.

Let us say that the current price at which the stock is trading is $14.50 for each share, but because of LEAPS, you can buy it at $17.50 for each share, and the premium for each share was $1.50. In that case, $19 per share is your breakeven point.

What Is the Working Mechanism of LEAPS?

You already read the example in the previous section; now if we are to continue it, this is how it can play –

- If the price at which the stock trades fall between $17.51 and $19, then you are going to incur some loss when after 2 years, the stock expires. Since $17.50 is your strike price and

the stock trades below this price, then the loss incurred will be 100%.
- If you notice that there has been a substantial rise in the price of the stocks, then you can close out on your position after informing your broker.
- The third option is you can find someone who will sell you the stock at a price of $17.50 per share. After that, if you choose to exercise the options, then you can go ahead and sell the shares at a price that is higher than what you bought them for. Let us assume the price rose to $25. The profit you will make is $6 for every share where $1.50 premium has been subtracted from the net capital gain of $7.50.

As you must have understood by now, the investment will be worthwhile if you predict that there will be a substantial rise in the price, something like $10 or $12 more than what it was, and it has to happen prior to the expiration date.

What Is the Result?

From the above example, it is clear that although you made an investment of only $1.50 for each share, you earned a profit of $6 for each share. Thus, by using the LEAPS strategy, you achieved a 400% gain from a stock rise of 72.4%. You definitely exposed yourself to a much higher level of risk, but since your prediction was correct, your risk was equally compensated for.

Now, if we multiple your gain of $6 per share with the 10,000 shares, it will amount to $60,000, and your investment at the beginning was $15,000.

Iron Condor

The possibility of making some profit is associated with almost every option strategy you come across. But along with the opportunity of making a good income, you also have the risk of incurring a loss. And that is exactly what trading is about. In short, if you have an expectation about getting a reward from a trade, you should also factor in the chances of loss when you initiate the trade.

There are certain traders who function under a market bias. They have this expectation about the market moving in a particular direction, and that is why they initiate a trade. These traders either adopt a strategy that is bearish or a bullish one.

And then there are other traders who do not operate under any kind of bias. There are two different ways in which they look at the market, and they are —

- They set for market-neutral strategies because they don't analyze the market with any preconceived notion about it.
- They intentionally choose market-neutral strategies because they expect a market that is non-directional and non-volatile.

The iron condor is one such market-neutral strategy. You can actually see the iron condor strategy is a simultaneous display of both out-of-the-money short call spread and out-of-the-money short put spread. When you learn more about this strategy, you will see that in this case, you get a net credit instantly, and that is why this strategy is also considered to be quiet attractive. Veterans and higher are usually the ones who should consider this strategy, and you should apply it when you think that within a specific time period, there will be minimal movement in the stock price. In simpler terms, if you are in search of a strategy with limited risk and yet you are already

Chapter 9: Bonus Strategies Explained

experienced with options trading, the iron condor will help you make the best out of low volatility.

Let's learn more about it.

How to Build an Iron Condor?

Let us start by seeing how you can construct this strategy. There are basically two vertical spreads that are combined together in this strategy. One of them is a bull put spread, and another one is a bear call spread. There are a total of 4 options contracts involved (all are different), but they have to possess different exercise prices and the same date of expiration.

The trader will have to sell an out-of-the-money put and an out-of-the-money call and, at the same time, buy a further out-of-the-money put and further out-of-the-money call in order to build the iron condor. If you look at the diagram of profit/loss for this particular strategy, you will notice that it actually looks similar to a bird with wings, and that's how it gets its name.

I know what you must be thinking – there are several strategies that are meant for the low-volatility markets, so why the iron condor? Well, the answer is quite simple. With this strategy, for the same amount of risk, you will have a large net credit on your plate. But no matter what, you should never overlook the other associated costs of the trade, which are mainly because of the sale of options and multiple purchases. In this case, the trade basically has four legs, and you have to consider the costs associated with them.

What Is the Objective of This Strategy?

Let us start by discussing who should consider opting for this strategy. If a trader wants to reduce their risk exposure and they are predicting that the price of the underlying asset is not going to go through much change before the date of expiration, then they should opt for this strategy. Like I mentioned previously, one of the major advantages of settling for this strategy is that you get to reduce your loss and, at the same time, yield a higher premium. Also, for any investment, the potential of return is much more because, in order to support the position, the margin requirement gets reduced to only one spread.

So, in short, this strategy can be defined as a limited-profit and limited-risk strategy that can help you

Chapter 9: Bonus Strategies Explained

make the best out of a non-volatile market. When you are constructing your position, the credit you receive is the maximum profit you can make out of this. This stage of maximum profit is attained when the price of the underlying stock at the time of expiration lies somewhere between the strike price of the put sold and the call. So, the formula will be something like this for maximum profits = The Total Premium Received – Total Commissions

Now, when do you think will you incur a loss with this strategy? Just like the profit potential, the potential for loss is also limited to a certain extend for an iron condor, but it is definitely more than the profit potential. When the price of the stock reduces, and it either stops at or goes below the purchased put's strike price, you incur a loss. Another case when you will incur a loss is when the price of the stock is equal increased to an equal level or goes above the purchased call's strike price. But no matter what the situation is, your maximum loss will be limited and it can be found out by finding the difference between the strike price of the calls and puts, and then you have to subtract the net premium that you had received when you entered into the trade.

Options Trading Crash Course

One of the most important aspects of using this strategy is that you should fully understand what the maximum potential loss and profit could be.

An Example of This Strategy

Let us say that the stocks of Company X are being traded at the price of $50 per share on December 1. You will have to start a multi-leg options strategy is you want to build an iron condor. In order to do that, you have to buy a January 40 put with $50 where each premium would be $0.50 (one contract has 100 shares) and another one of January 60 call with $50 and premium of $0.50. And, simultaneously, for a credit of $100, you have to sell one January 45 put and January 55 call both of which would have a premium of $1 (100 shares x $1 premium).

At the outset of the trade, the trader will get a total of $100. Do you know how? By selling the 55 call and the 45 put, the trader will get $200, and you have to subtract the $100, which was utilized for buying the 60 call and the 40 put. This $100 is actually the maximum profit potential after implementing this strategy. If the price of the underlying stock on the date of expiration reaches a level between the inner sold options, that is, the 55 call and the 45 put, the trader will realize the maximum profit. This is because, in such a case, the options will become worthless on expiration, and the trader will be keeping the premium.

Now, let us see when the trader might incur a loss. The breakeven points for this trade is $44-$56, and if the stock closes beyond this range in any way, then the trader will incur a loss. For example, if the price became $40, then except for the sold 45 put, all the options will be expiring worthless. The 45 put will be of $5 value to the person who sold it (a contract has 100 shares). The loss that the trader will have to bear is $400 (subtract the $100 credit from the total loss of $500 on the 45 put).

Bull or Bear Spread

You probably already know this, but I am going to explain it once more just for the sake of this strategy. When a trader believes that the price of an underlying asset is going to increase and will continue doing so, then the trader is bullish on the price. On the other hand, when the trader believes that the price of an underlying asset is going to decrease and will keep falling further, then the trader is bearish on the price. Depending on the pricing opinions they have, the traders make their decisions accordingly.

Both investors and traders have numerous ways of determining when they want to sell an option, and when they want to buy depending on how they view the market. And the bear and bull spread are just two such methods. With the help of the bull spread, the chances of incurring risk while making a profit are reduced. On the contrary, a bear spread is implemented for minimizing the losses, especially when prices are dropping and also maximized profit in the process.

Both call and put options are present in bear and bull spread. But the effects of these options in case of these strategies are different on every trader and their capital.

How Does The Bull Spread Work?

When the bull spread strategy involves the use of call options, it is referred to as the bull call spread, and similarly, it is referred to as the bull put spread when it involves the use of put options. I know you must be wondering what the difference between the two is — the basic difference lies in the cash flow timing.

Chapter 9: Bonus Strategies Explained

Let us discuss the bull call spread first – the payment is made upfront, and when the option expires, you seek profit. In the case of the bull put spread, it is quite the opposite – the money is collected beforehand, and the aim of the trader is to hold on to that money as much as he/she can at the time of its expiration. In this case, the profit potential is not limited. If the price of the underlying asset goes above the strike price and the option's premium, your profit would not be limited. But if the price goes below the strike price, then the premium that you had initially paid will be the loss you incur.

But in both cases, the sale of options is giving you a premium, so if you had to purchase the options on their own, then it would have required you more money than the initial cash investment in this strategy. So, the bull spread is basically an optimistic strategy and is applied when you predict there will be a rise in the underlying's assets price.

How Does the Bear Spread Work?

The bear spread strategy is implemented when you expect the underlying security's price to decline. So, you might either think about protecting your current position, or you can aim to make a profit. Just like the bull spread, you can categorize the bear spread into two categories – bear call spread and bear put spread, both of which fall under the category of vertical spreads.

Let us start by discussing the bear put first. You will start by buying a put because you are predicting a decline in the price and you intend to make a profit from it. Then, you will sell that put at a strike price lower than before but having the same expiration date. When your strategy is successful, the cost of buying the put will be met, and you will incur a net debit.

Now, let's see what happens in the case of a bear call spread. In order to generate profit, the trader will write a call and then buy a call that has a higher strike price but the same expiry date because this will limit the risk exposure. When this strategy is successful, the trader will get a net credit.

Now that you know the basics, there is one more thing that you should know about these spreads, that is, they are classified into either credit spreads or debit spreads. The bear put spreads, and the bull call spreads are where the premiums are paid and so they are debit spreads. On the other hand, the bear call spreads, and the bull put spreads are where the premiums are collected, and hence, they are credit spreads.

Married Put

This options trading strategy involves the purchase of an at-the-money put option and, at the same time, purchasing an equal number of shares for the underlying asset. This strategy aims to shield the price of the stock from any depreciation. The major benefit of using this strategy is that even in the worst scenario, you will be losing some part of the money. The major disadvantage is the premium of the put option, which is quite significant. The strategy can even be implemented on stocks that have low volatility, and investors are predicting a drastic change in price because of some announcement.

How Does the Strategy Work?

You can say that the married put is somewhat like an insurance policy that options traders should have. If you are worried that the stock might run into some complexities in the near future then you use the married put. It is basically a bullish strategy. When you own the stock, and you have implemented the protective put option, you can still practice your right to vote or receive dividends but on the other hand, if you had just went for a call option, then the stock ownership benefits might not have been the same as now.

The profit potential for both long call and married put is unlimited because the underlying stock's price can rise as high as it wants. This is also the reason why the term synthetic long call is often used to refer to the married put. In order to reach the breakeven point while implementing this strategy, when the premium you paid for the options contract is equal to the rise in the price of the stock. Whenever it crosses this level, it will be considered your profit. The risk associated with this strategy is limited to the premium you had paid along with the commissions. When the long put's strike price is either equal to or more than the price of the underlying asset, that is when the maximum loss occurs.

Now, you must be wondering when you can use this strategy. In order to understand that, you have to realize that the married put is more like a capital-preserving strategy and less of a profit-making strategy. So, when you are trading a bullish stock, and you think that there might be some uncertainty in the near future, that is when you should implement the strategy. For the traders who are new to the market, they prefer this strategy because of the limited loss associated with it gives them peace of mind.

An Example of This Strategy

Let us assume that a trader is interested in an ABC stock and purchases 100 shares priced at $20 per share. The trader also purchases an ABC $17.50 put at $0.50 ($0.50 x 100 shared = $50). So, the trader has secured a stock position for himself and has also invested in an insurance policy for his position in the form of the put so that if the price of the stock falls below $17.50 before the expiration date, the trader's position will remain protected. But for this put to be considered as married put, the stock and the put has to be purchased on the same day, and the trader should also give instructions to his broker saying that if it comes to a situation where the put is exercised, the stock will be delivered.

Protective Collar Strategy

When the market is highly volatile and undergoes huge swings, every trader looks for safety and implements strategies accordingly. The protective collar is one such strategy you apply for short-term downside protection. On using this strategy, you will be able to use it in your favor when the market moves in the upward direction and also find a way in which your losses will be protected. At times, this strategy doesn't require any cost or very little cost.

The strategy consists of both a put option and a call option. The main aim of the put option is to hedge the risk associated with the stock, and the call option is used to finance the purchase of the put. So, you can also see this strategy as a combination of a long put and a covered call.

Both the options in this strategy are used when they are out-of-the-money, but they should contain an equal number of contracts and have the same date of expiration. Now, since the strategy is meant to provide downside protection to the underlying asset until it reaches its expiration date, it is known as the protective put.

Chapter 9: Bonus Strategies Explained

Now that we have established the fact that the main reason people use the protective collar is to hedge the risk away, you should have also understood by now that the strike price of the purchased put should be lower than the strike price of the written call. So, if we say that a particular stock is trading at $40, then the strike price of the written call should be something like $42.50, whereas the purchased put should have a strike price like $37.50. The strike price of the call basically acts as a cap on the potential profit because if the trade goes beyond that level, it might be called off. Similarly, the strike price of the put offers a downside limit for the stock, thus minimizing your losses below that level.

When Should You Use This Strategy?

If a trader wants medium-term or short-term downside protection and at the same time, they do not want to spend too much money on it, then the protective collar is what they should go for. Now, as you know it can be quite expensive to purchase protective puts, but that cost can be reduced substantially by investing in out-of-the-money calls. That is why it is said that you do not really require any cost for constructing this strategy or in fact, you might be able to produce a net credit out of it.

But the major disadvantage of using this strategy is that you will have to compromise on your upside in order to gain protection. So, if the stock price takes a hit and reduces, the protective collar can really of great help, but on the contrary, if the stock price increases, this strategy is going to cap your profits. Whatever gain you get above the strike price of the call will no longer be yours. So, if we follow the example that I mentioned earlier, if the stock price increases to $45 where the strike price of the call was $42.50, the call will be surrendered at the strike price, and anything above that will be a waste. So, you have to give up a profit of $2.50. So, if the stock rose to $55, then you will have to give up a profit of $12.50.

So now you must be wondering which market condition would be ideal for implementing this strategy. Well, they usually do well in broad markets. You can also use them when certain stocks are displaying signs of retreating way in advance. If you are currently in a strongly bullish market, be very careful while implementing the strategy because it is highly likely that the stocks will be called away in such a situation, and the upside of your portfolio will become capped.

Chapter 9: Bonus Strategies Explained

An Example of This Strategy

Let us see how you can construct this strategy for the company ABC. The company closed on Feb 12 at $177.09. Now, suppose you have 100 shares of the company, and you had purchased them at $90. So, the stock has undergone a rise of 97% from the price at which you had purchased it. In such a case, in order to protect your profits, you can implement the protective collar.

Your first step would be to write a covered call on your current position. Let us assume that in the month of March, the trading price of the $185 calls is $3.65/$3.75 and so you write a contract. This will give you $365 (minus the commissions) as your premium income. At the same time, you also buy a contract of $170 puts in the month of March, whose trading price is at $4.35/$4.50. So, to buy the puts, you will have to pay $450 and any commission. Thus, if we keep the commissions aside, constructing the collar strategy will require you an investment of $85. Now, let us see what different scenarios can play from here –

- The stocks are trading at $187 (more than $185) before the expiration date

Now, in this scenario, a price of at least $2 would be maintained for the $185 call, whereas it will be probably close to zero for the $170 put. Since you have a premium income of $3.65, you can close your short call position but in the event that you don't want to do it and you want the shares to be called away at $185, your net profit would be $9,415 because [($185 - $90) - $0.85 collar's net cost] x 100 shares gives $9,415. But remember how I said one of the downsides of this strategy is that your profit is capped. So, if you had not used the strategy in this case, your profit could have been $9,700 because ($187 - $90) x 100 shares.

- The stocks are trading at $165 (less than $170 before the expiration date

In this case, the puts would be somewhere around $5, whereas the calls would be almost zero. So, what you do is that you sell the shares you own at $165 so that you can keep a profit of $7,915 as [($170 - $90) - $0.85 net cost of the collar] x 100 gives this amount. But if you had not used the strategy, you would have made a profit of $7,500, which $415 less than what you made with the strategy.

Chapter 9: Bonus Strategies Explained

- The stocks are trading at $177 (that is between $185 and $170) before the expiration date

In this case, both options will be close to zero when they are trading. The unrealized gain in such a scenario would be $8,700 [($177 - $90) x 100 shares], but you also have to adjust the $85 that you had to bear while you implemented the strategy and so after subtracting the amount, your net profit would be $8,615.

Chapter 10: Common Mistakes Beginners Make and How to Avoid Them

Options trading is basically every trader's point of interest, and you can make handsome profits from it too. If you have come this far in the book, then you already know the potential that this field has, but if you make the wrong trades, it can be equally devastating for your career. So, if you want to take this seriously, here are some mistakes that are commonly made, and once you know them beforehand, you will think twice before making them yourselves.

Not Having a Trading Plan

Not following any plan for trading is probably the most common mistake of all, especially among the beginners. It might be that you read in some finance magazine that a particular company's stocks are performing well, or maybe you got a tip at a random gathering, and you decided to act it. Well, should you? The answer is both yes and no. No, because you should never take anyone on their word when it

Chapter 10: Common Mistakes Beginners Make and How to Avoid Them

comes to trading. Yes, because it might actually turn out to be a good tip in certain cases, but you first have to perform quick research of your own and then decide whether that tip would be worth believing or not.

If you do not have a trading plan before you dive into the world of options trading, it is simply as if you are driving your car, and yet you do not have a license. So, when you face a situation of crisis, the losses can be huge. In options, you do not have all the time in the world. There is a fixed amount of time within which you have to take action; otherwise, your option will expire worthless. You always have to be alert for any opportunities that might come your way, and if there is an opportunity, don't ever miss it. So, your goal of making a lot of money might not just be in your favor just because you did not make a plan for it. Remember that no matter how good your strategy is, sometimes even they can fail when you do not have a trading plan.

Some of the things that your trading plan should definitely possess are the type of options that you are particularly interested in like Nifty, equity, commodities, and so on, the amount of money that you can afford to invest in trading on a monthly basis, the amount of money you want to invest in each trade, your risk appetite, and your expected returns from a trade. Make sure that this plan is followed for every trade that you conduct. You will be getting temptations of going off the track, but you have to resist those temptations and prevent yourself from risking too much. Your fear and greed both have to be controlled if you want to make it big. If you are just a beginner, start small and then work your way up to the top slowly and steadily.

Believing In the One-Size-Fits-All Concept

Selecting the strategy that would work best for you depending upon the situation of the market is what options trading is all about. Suppose you figured out a good strategy, and you have been using it for quite some time, and it is working out well for you. But that specific strategy is not meant for all types of trades. For example, you cannot use strategies of a bullish market in a bearish one. So, if you keep repeating your strategy without even evaluating the trades, thinking that it will work like some magic wand and make you win every trade, then you are wrong. You

Chapter 10: Common Mistakes Beginners Make and How to Avoid Them

have to learn to predict the market outlook and then choose the strategy that is best for you.

You have to perform technical analysis and fundamental analysis to find out which strategies you should use. Both macro and microeconomic factors have to be taken into consideration. Gather knowledge from different places by reading books and going to workshops. Read the views of experts from different reputed finance magazines. After you have figured out the market outlook, picking the right strategy would become much easier.

You have already read about the important strategies in the book, and you know when you have to apply each of them. That is why it is important that you read the previous chapters before stepping into the world of trading.

Ignoring the Expiration Date

The expiration date of options is one of the major factors affecting our trades. As you know that in order to make profits, you have to speculate on the direction of the stock movement. Well, at the same time, I am also asking you to speculate how much time is it going to take a particular point because, in the case of options where your time is limited by expiration date, it cannot take you forever. Let us say that you researched and found some factors that can positively impact the price of the stock, but do you, when that price is going to reach the level you want it to reach?

Trading does not only mean looking after strategies. In the case of options, you have to look out for the expiration dates as well. Just like the strategies, when it comes to the expiration date, you have a multitude of choices for it too. But you know, once you have gone through the previous point, that is, once you have built your market outlook, settling for the right expiration date kind of becomes the easy task. There are some questions that you should keep in your checklist because then it becomes to figure it out. For example, you can ask yourself how much time do you think a particular trade will need in order to play out. You can also ask yourself whether you want to hold a trade through major events or not like a stock split or a public announcement. Lastly, you should also ask yourself whether you have the required liquidity to pursue after this.

Chapter 10: Common Mistakes Beginners Make and How to Avoid Them

Overleveraging the Trades

It is always advised to beginners to get used to stock investment before you start options trading. When you have done stocks investing first, it is more likely for you to have handled huge amounts of money directly, and in fact, buying stocks directly also means that you have to pay the entire share price.
So, for this example, let us say that you are a person who has the capability of buying stocks worth $1000 at a time, and let's say that you have done this before but not in options. Now that you have switched over to the options because of their cheap nature and that they are a derivative. If you had to buy the underlying asset directly with all your money, it would have cost you way more money than what you're investing in purchasing the options. So, you don't need to invest a thousand dollars for purchasing that many amount of stocks in the form of options contracts.

But this also poses a risk — a risk where you might end up overleveraging. Leverage is a powerful tool only when you use it wisely. So, just because there is leverage doesn't mean that you should invest more amount than necessary.

That is why there is a very common rule that is followed – consider it as a rule of thumb in your case. Try and limit your loss to within 5% for every trade that you do. This is something that you have to strictly abide by so that all your capital is not lost behind any particular trade. When you lose only some money in a trade, you can always pick yourself back up and invest in a different trade, which brings me to the next point.

Error In Position Sizing of Your Trades

There are two common emotions that are responsible for all errors related to position sizing. These emotions are greed and fear. Suppose you are making a decision, and you become too greedy about your profits, then it might happen that you position your trade too big that it is not right for the size of the account that you have. And this is even more common when your outlook of the market is wrong and then what you get in return is not profit but a crippling loss recovering from which can become really difficult.

This was just one mistake of position sizing. The other one is when you position your trade too small. There

Chapter 10: Common Mistakes Beginners Make and How to Avoid Them

is nothing wrong with trading small, but do you know what it means? It means that you might not get the chance to make any substantial profit at all.

Here are some common ways in which you can maintain appropriate position sizing —

- Make sure the risk percentage for each trade is somewhere around 1-5% of your total account value.
- For every trade, it is better that you stick to a consistent dollar value like $100 or $1000 based on how much you can afford to risk.

No matter what you do or which strategy you use, your position sizing should be such that you are comfortable risking that amount of money. In simpler terms, even if the trade does not happen like you predicted it to be, it won't hurt you to lose the money invested. In the ideal case, your trade value should be such that it is meaningful enough, but not too big that it has reason to make you lose your sleep at night.

Buying Options Based On Whether They Are Cheap or Not

Human beings tend to think that whenever something is cheap, it is better to buy it rather than going for something that is costly. They think that this is the most cost-effective thing to do. But what you don't understand is that with options, following this 'cheap' tactic is not going to help you. In fact, it is going to ruin your trade. It is usually said that an option tends to be more out-of-the-money when it's premium is more towards the lower side. Yes, at first glance, it might appear to you that you have just found the biggest steal of your life but trust me when I say this, don't fall for the trap because even if you get it, making any money with the help of that option would be highly unlikely.

When the premiums of options are towards the lower side, the strike price of those options is usually either well below or well above the market price. In simpler words, if you had to make money with such an option, then there has to be a miraculous change in the price for you to do so. So, let us say you bought a call option that has a very low premium, but if you want to make money with it, it has to show a drastic movement upward. Similarly, there has to be a drastic movement downward if you want to make money after buying a put option with a low premium.

Chapter 10: Common Mistakes Beginners Make and How to Avoid Them

So, in these deals, making money is not really in the picture unless and until there is a big announcement or a big earnings report on the way. But by this, I do not mean that you are not going to get any profits with any of the out-of-the-money options. You can make money with them but not with this strategy, and also, as a beginner, you should try to steer clear of the out-of-the-money options.

Lack of Knowledge Regarding Early-Assigned Options

There is something not many options traders understand in the beginning, and that is – when you are selling an option, it is no longer a right but an obligation. If the contract has been assigned by the buyer, you will have to sell or buy based on the contract, and your hands are tied here. Let us say that you are selling a call; in that case, the stock has to be sold at the strike price. On the other hand, if you are selling a put, the stock will have to be bought at the strike price.

Investors who do exercise their option early usually fall into the clutches of panic, and they cannot figure out what to do with the option, and so, they think exercising it would be the best way out. But there are investors who are able to identify when it would be the best solution because you have to cut off your losses. No matter what it is, it is something that you have to prepare yourself for; otherwise, you will end up making the wrong decision. In order to possess the underlying asset or cover the transaction that you are about to make, you have to possess sufficient cash. So, if you don't plan for this circumstance, you are going to be caught off-guard and left high and dry.

Not Using the Concept of Probability

Now, we move on to the next common mistake that is made by beginners when they step into the world of options trading. When you are placing a trade, taking the probabilities into consideration is a very important task. But if you fail to do so, then you will also have to reap the consequences of it. When you take the probability factor, you are actually doing a statistical analysis of what might happen in the market, and this will also clarify the risk-to-reward ratio of your trade. You have to keep in mind that

Chapter 10: Common Mistakes Beginners Make and How to Avoid Them

there is no directional bias involved when it comes to probability. It simply assesses the current factors in the market and then performs an evaluation to show the level of price at any date before the expiration of the option. In fact, in order to make this determination, you can take the help of your trading platform because most of them are going to provide you with a probability calculator, and if you are not sure whether they provide it or not, make sure you ask them before opening an account.

Facing Loss Because You Chose to Stay In a Written Option

Let me make one thing very clear to every one of you – you have bought an option, and that doesn't mean that you have to ride it for the entire duration of time. If the option is going to be 'in-the-money' when it expires, you can choose to get out of it by selling it. You have to remember that when you are trading options, you are taking a scientific approach, and it is not the same as gambling. Your hope should not be that when the expiration date approaches, your option expires, and you are left with the premium that you paid. There are so many cases when just before expiration, the option took a sudden turn in the wrong direction overnight, and the investor incurred a heavy loss.

If there is a decrease in the price of the stock and I am talking about a written put, then you have to know this that you will be losing a lot of money on it. Don't forget that you are under the obligation to purchase the stock at its strike price, which would mean that you will face a huge loss.

So, you have to take the better path and buy your way out of the option rather than just sitting on it the entire time. In fact, you might even get to keep some of the premium especially when you sell it for a higher price, and the premium is only a fraction of that price. This is how you cut off your losses and not sit on the. You will have to subtract the commissions from the premium and keep the rest of the money. So now, you would not be left with a huge loss because you are under no obligation to purchase the stock at any predetermined price.

Here is a rule of thumb that you should follow in these situations. If you see that you are left with around 80% of the premium that you had initially

Chapter 10: Common Mistakes Beginners Make and How to Avoid Them

paid, even after buying yourself out, then you should definitely go for it. This is the best way out in these situations because you are not only walking away from the risk, but you still have the money in your wallet.

You Double Up to Cover Your Losses

This is something I have seen so many beginners doing, but remember, you never know how options are going to turn. No matter how good your strategies are, whenever you incur a loss, you will panic, and that panic itself can make you turn in the wrong direction and implement wrong strategies. So, you cannot let your emotions control you when you are trading.

The most common mistake or result of such a panicky situation is that people think about doubling up, and this leads to far greater losses. This, in turn, puts you in front of greater risks. In fact, if you don't perform sufficient market research and the stock continues to move further in the wrong direction, then your losses are going to double up too. So, you have to perform a reevaluation of your trading strategy and cut your losses.

Not Having an Exit Strategy

Most beginners don't understand the importance of an exit plan, and so they choose to ignore it. Not having an exit strategy is mostly because they have not set any target for loss or profit and so they are not sure as to how much money they want to take home from any particular trade. They are not sure as to how much loss they can withstand or even afford to absorb. They are totally unaware of whether they want their options to expire and become worthless or whether they want to exercise the options because the expiration date comes. You need an exit plan if you want to build it, you will have to know all of the things that I mentioned above.

As you know, options trading is time-bound, and that is why it becomes all the more essential for you to have an exit strategy. In the case of stocks, even if things are not going like you had planned for them to go, you can wait for some time to see how things are played and recover. Moreover, in the case of expiring

Chapter 10: Common Mistakes Beginners Make and How to Avoid Them

options, there is a difference when it comes to taxation.

So, your exit strategy has to be in place even before you start your trades. And once you have figured out what your exit strategy is going to be, do not deviate from the path. No matter what happens, you have to stick to the exit strategy. You also have to target a point which will serve as your maximum losses. This should be the amount that you can absorb. If you find that your trade has hit that point, you need to come out of it. Resist your temptation to wait and see how it turns out because you might end up losing all your money instead.

Trading Options That Are Illiquid

You should focus on trading options that have a higher level of liquidity. This is because options trading is more of a short-term thing, and if your assets don't have the required liquidity, they cannot be traded as fast as you want them to. In fact, this becomes even more important when you are focusing on cutting off your losses. If the option that you have is illiquid, then you will require more time to buy yourself out of it and so cutting off your losses will not be as easy as you want it to be.

The open interest is something you have to pay attention to when you are trading options. If you don't know what it means well open interest refers to the number of contracts that are open at that particular strike price. It is will be in your favor when the open interest is more. And the same property applies for volume too. It is somewhat similar to what happens in the case of stocks. It is better when the volume of trades is more for any particular day. So, if you want your exit strategy to be good, you should be looking at a higher volume.

If we are to speak generally, then I would say illiquid options are more in the case of smaller companies, and liquid options are more in the case of bigger companies.

Lastly, I want to remind you that mistakes are common in trading. It happens with everyone. In fact, anyone who is well-established as a trader today has made plenty of mistakes, but you should focus on managing your risk and enhancing your knowledge about the market. In case a mistake occurs, don't be

Chapter 10: Common Mistakes Beginners Make and How to Avoid Them

too harsh on yourself. In case you are a beginner and have not tried options trading before, I think you should try your hand at paper trading first so that you totally understand what it is all about.

Conclusion

Thank you for making it through to the end of *Options Trading Crash Course*, let's hope it was informative and able to provide you with all of the tools you need to achieve your goals whatever they may be.

I hope this book has been able to provide you the answers to all the questions that you had in mind. So, don't worry too much and dive into the world of options trading right away. The world of options trading is very vast, and there is always something new to learn. You have to first focus on mastering the tactics you have learned in this book and then move on to acquire some more advanced strategies. If you want your trading career to be successful, you have to know the ins and outs of options trading by heart, and you have to understand that it will take some time.

There is potential to carve out a full-time career from trading, but for that, you have to keep at it no matter how many failures you face. No one makes it big in the stock market overnight. It takes time and patience, and you will surely achieve your goals if you are persistent. You have to learn to mitigate your risks

Conclusion

and assess your situation with a clear mind so that you don't bite more than you can eat. Trading is not an easy business, and when it comes to the long haul, most people don't have the patience for it. But if you have read this book, you already know what awaits you at the other end if you learn options trading and start placing your trades. But educate yourself on the risks you are taking and don't give in to greed.

Finally, if you found this book useful in any way, a review on Amazon is always appreciated!

Glossary

Here is a list of common terms that you have come across in this book, and I am quickly going to provide you the definition of all of them.

Breakeven Point

The price of the underlying asset at which the strategy will neither give you loss nor profit at the time of expiration is termed as the breakeven point.

Call Option

With the help of the call option, a trader obtains the right to purchase a total of 100 shares at a certain price, which is termed as the strike price, which will be deemed worthless after a certain date known as the expiration date.

Commission

When the brokerage firm charges a certain amount of fee for the services that it has provided, this fee is termed as commission.

Glossary

Covered Call

When a call option is sold, and it is done against the current position of the stock, the call option is termed as a covered call.

Credit Transaction

When a stock or option is sold, the money that you receive in your account from this sale is referred to as the credit transaction. Some strategies involve multiple parts, and in such a case, you will see the term net credit transaction being used, which means that the total cash amount that was paid is lesser than the total cash amount that was credited.

Debit Transaction

When a stock or option is purchased, the money that is paid to complete the transaction is referred to as a debit transaction. When there are multiple parts involved in a transaction, you will see the term net debit transaction being used, which means that the total cash amount that you had received was lesser than the total cash amount that you had paid.

ETF or Exchange Traded Fund

This is a particular type of security that shows that you own the shares in a particular fund or trust in which several component stocks are present. Just like stocks, ETFs are not only listed on the security exchanges but are also traded.

Exercise

This is the process by which the terms of the option contract are invoked by the option buyer. So, when a contract is being exercised, it means that the call owners will purchase the underlying asset, and the put owners will sell the underlying asset. Options contracts are automatically exercised when at the time of expiration, they are in-the-money.

Expiration Date

The day beyond which you cannot exercise the option is known as the expiration date.

Extrinsic Value

Glossary

When an option is in-the-money, the portion of the premium that is greater than the intrinsic value is referred to as the extrinsic value. The entire premium of the option is its extrinsic value when the option is OTM or out-of-the-money.

Hedging

This is basically a conservative and risk management strategy that is implemented to reduce the risk in the investment through a transaction that will balance your current position.

Historical Volatility

Historical volatility is the volatility of a particular asset as measured over a certain period of time be it a quarter, month, or year.

Implied Volatility

When the present market price of the underlying asset predicts or implies the volatility of the asset in the future, it is referred to as implied volatility.

Intrinsic Value

In case an option is exercised at a certain point of time, the profit that can be obtained from such a transaction is termed as the intrinsic value, and so the underlying asset is either sold or bought at the present market price. An option is termed as ITM or in-the-money when it's intrinsic value is positive, and it is termed as OTM or out-of-the-money when it's intrinsic value is negative.

Premium

Premium is simply the price of an option, and it usually represents the entire dollar value of the contract and not the price-per-share.

Put Option

With the help of the put option, a trader obtains the right to sell a total of 100 shares at a certain price, which is termed as the strike price, which will be deemed worthless after a certain date known as the expiration date.

Strike Price

Glossary

The price that is determined for the traders at which they can sell the put options or buy call options of any particular stock is termed as the strike price.

Time Decay

Since options are not valid endlessly and they operate within a fixed range of date called the expiration date, with each passing day, the time value starts eroding towards zero, and this process of erosion is termed as time decay.

Time Value

The amount by which the intrinsic value is less than that of the market price of the option is its time value.

www.ingramcontent.com/pod-product-compliance
Lightning Source LLC
Chambersburg PA
CBHW071407210526
45465CB00001B/282